MYS[illegible] STALKS THE PRAIRIE

UNEXPLAINED CATTLE KILLINGS AND UFOS IN MONTANA

UPDATED AND EXPANDED EDITION, FEATURING:

An introduction by Joan Bird,
author of *Montana UFOS and Extraterrestrials*

An epilogue by author Keith Wolverton

An interview with author Keith Wolverton
and Montana sheriff Pete Howard

KEITH WOLVERTON
WITH ROBERTA DONOVAN
PHOTOGRAPHS BY KEN ANDERSON

RIVERBEND
PUBLISHING

Mystery Stalks the Prairie

ISBN: 978-1-60639-122-8

Printed in the USA

1 2 3 4 5 6 7 8 MG 26 25 24 23 22 21

Cover and text design by Sarah Cauble, sarahcauble.com

Riverbend Publishing
P.O. Box 5833
Helena, MT 59604
1-406-449-0200
riverbendpublishing.com

Regarding the Updated Edition of *Mystery Stalks the Prairie*

This edition contains a verbatim copy of the original book, *Mystery Stalks the Prairie,* published in 1976, including the original photographs.

It also contains three features that update and expand the book:

An epilogue by author Keith Wolverton, written in 2019, that describes his experiences with UFOs and other phenomena since the publication of *Mystery Stalks the Prairie*, and his conclusions about such phenomena.

A transcript of a 2016 YouTube interview with Keith Wolverton and retired sheriff Pete Howard, who worked with Wolverton in the 1970s. In the interview, Wolverton and Howard expand on the cattle mutilations described in the book, and they reveal remarkable UFO incidents that occurred at the same time, including a saucer-shaped UFO flying alongside an Air Force bomber, UFOs hovering above nuclear missile sites, and the government confiscation of radar evidence of a UFO.

An introduction by Joan Bird, author of *Montana UFOs and Extraterrestrials*, that describes the impact of the original publication of *Mystery Stalks the Prairie*, the current status of UFOs and cattle mutilations, and a report of a cattle mutilation on a Montana Indian reservation in 1947.

CONTENTS

INTRODUCTION

to the Updated Edition

Joan Bird
Author of *Montana UFOs and Extraterrestrials*

My dog-eared, soiled, chewed, and well-traveled copy of *Mystery Stalks the Prairie* came to me fairly early in my plunge into UFO literature, a gift from a friend who had lived in Choteau, Montana, and was moving out of state. At that time, checking on its availability, I saw one used copy online for $35. Later I couldn't find a copy for under $100, and currently I can find no copies online of the original 1976 publication.

Mystery Stalks the Prairie is a classic, the first book published on the subject, cited and credited in every cattle mutilation book since. It's an undeniably well-researched and important book in the documentation of these mysterious cattle deaths and associated unexplained phenomena. I'm pleased that Keith lived to see what a valuable contribution his investigation and resultant book was to understanding a disturbing phenomenon, and that he was able to be involved in the planning of this updated edition. I'm sorry that Roberta Donovan is no longer around, as she deserves major credit for her key role in the excellent writing and editing of the book.

I met Keith in the late 1980s or early 1990s when I was working for The Nature Conservancy in Helena, Montana. The state director had friends who had worked on a Cascade County Crime Attack Team with Keith Wolverton around 1978. Ray Worring, a psychologist interested in ESP, and his ranching friend, Whit Hibbard, trained the officers in the use of hypnosis to access additional memories in witnesses, and later developed a manual on psychic forensics based on their successful use of psychics in solving criminal investigations. Ray was always interested in finding people with psychic gifts and cultivating those abilities, using field trips to pictographs, petroglyphs, stone rings, and other formations.

On one of those trips, I met Keith Wolverton. He had with him a smooth, oblong, cylindrical stone about 15 inches long, loaned to him by a woman who felt it was the cause of strange occurrences and sounds. Psychometry is the ability to get intuitive or psychic information from an object by holding it and tuning in to it. The stone was incredibly symmetric, and we all felt it was not a simple river stone, but we had no conclusive answers for Keith. Later, George McMullen, a highly gifted psychic who was regularly employed by law enforcement and archaeologists, used psychometry with the stone. He believed it was naturally formed through unusual conditions, perhaps being rolled under a waterfall, but that it had been used in ceremonies by indigenous people, and that could explain some of the strange phenomena associated with it.

At that early meeting with Keith, I heard about his book on cattle mutilations and UFOs, and his connection with Ray and Whit in investigating strange, unexplained phenomena. I was impressed with Keith's reserved and professional demeanor. He clearly took the use of intuition and psychic forensics seriously as one avenue of investigation.

Whit knew Keith well and considered him one of the most honest people he had ever met. "Those guys are trained to be skeptical," Whit said. "He had a highly tuned B.S. detector. Came from his law enforcement training, and wasn't afraid to call people on it. He was not prone to exaggeration or hysteria but was very objective."

Whit once asked Keith if he believed this "alien" stuff, that extraterrestrials (ETs) were responsible for the cattle mutilations. Keith replied that in some of the cases, the evidence was compelling, but that he really didn't have an *a priori* belief one way or another.

In 2008, shortly after signing the contract to write a book on Montana UFOs and extraterrestrials, I met Keith for lunch in Great Falls, Montana. I'd heard he had been to the Skinwalker Ranch in Utah and was curious about what he had experienced. He said he went there with researcher Colm Kelleher and George Knapp of KLAS-TV in Las Vegas. Keith had heard there was some strange stuff going on there, but nothing unusual happened in that visit. (George Knapp is widely recognized for his investigations and expertise in UFOs and secret government projects, especially at Area 51 and the Skinwalker Ranch.) Colm Kelleher worked for Robert Bigelow of Bigelow Aerospace in his research institute, National Institute for Discovery Science (NIDS.) Colm once took Keith into a room at NIDS that had a big map of Montana; the map showed the locations of all the cattle mutilation cases in Keith's investigations.

In 2017, mainstream news reported that Bigelow had a contract with the $22 million Pentagon UFO investigation project, 2007-2012, called the Advance Aerial Threat Identification Program (AATIP), with congressional funding initiated by Senators Harry Reid, Ted Stevens, and Daniel Inouye. Reid knew of Bigelow's interest in the subject of UFOs and no doubt had something to do with Bigelow winning the contract. In a 2017 interview on the television news program *60 Minutes*, Bigelow responded to the question, do you believe UFOs have come to Earth, by saying: "There has been and is an existing presence on Earth, an ET presence."

The revelation of the secret Pentagon UFO research program in the *New York Times* (December 16, 2017) was a major breakthrough of government secrecy, and while admissions are still limited, mainstream news reports indicate a new era of at least partial disclosure of what the government actually knows. It is highly likely that Keith's investigations and Kelleher's maps may be part of the extensive classified reports purported to have come from Bigelow's contract, and not yet released to the public.

When I asked Keith over lunch that day what he thought now about ETs and cattle mutilations, he said he still didn't really know. He did say that some government agency was interested in receiving all of his reports, but when he asked his contacts there about what they knew, he was stonewalled.

Realizing just how important and groundbreaking Keith's work and book were, retired anesthesiologist Dr. Richard O'Connor arranged an interview in August 2016 with Keith and another member of his investigative team from the 1970s, retired Sheriff and Justice of the Peace, Pete Howard. Dr. O' Connor was a close associate and friend of Dr. Jesse Marcel, a doctor and surgeon whose father was one of the first people on the Roswell UFO crash. O'Connor founded the Jesse A. Marcel Memorial Library in Helena, Montana, to make UFO and extraterrestrial information readily available to people interested in the subject. His video of these two retired sheriffs talking about the cattle mutilation investigation and their experiences at that time has been viewed by hundreds of thousands of people, and a transcript of that interview is included in this book.

So, in the 45 years since *Mystery* was published, what have we learned about cattle mutilations? They are still happening, though not as frequently as during the years of Keith's investigations from 1974 to 1976. UFO researcher William Puckett has a Montana UFO website with a cattle mutilation page. The most recent reports on his website are from 2013 in Browning and 2012 in Polson. His website is: ufosightingsmontana.com/category/cattle-mutilations-montana/

Retired Montana Sheriff and Justice of the Peace Pete Howard reports that the last one he had heard about was in the Dupuyer area in 2020, but they had been getting two or three reports every year for several years before that, also in the Dupuyer area.

Recent reports have come from all over Montana, as well as Oregon, Kansas, Colorado, and New Mexico, the latter two states having an especially long history of activity.

Theories abound as to the purpose of these mutilations. I believe readers will agree that Keith's investigations effectively eliminate animal predators as the cause. Satanic cults have also been considered, as law enforcement does occasionally get wind of cult activity. One time Keith and Whit drove up to Calgary, Alberta, to see what the RCMP were thinking. Those officers believed satanic cults were the cause and reported finding the anesthetic Ketamine in a carcass. However, the fact that there are many UFO reports at the same time as the mutilations, and that mutilated cattle have been dropped onto the ground from a height above, and a consistent lack of footprints at the mutilation sites, rules out cults, at least as the sole explanation. There is general agreement that unusual aircraft and advanced technologies are involved in many cases.

Dr. Steven Greer, a longtime UFO researcher, originator of the Disclosure Project, and UFO documentary producer, has met with hundreds of military and intelligence witnesses.

In May 2001, he brought together 22 of those highly credentialed and credible witnesses for a National Press Club Conference that was largely ignored and ridiculed by mainstream news. Greer believes that the UFOs involved in abductions and cattle mutilation are actually our military's advanced spacecraft, and that they use cyborgs or small humans in alien disguise to instill public fear of aliens. To be sure, there are a growing number of witnesses who say that the United States has been building advanced spacecraft since the 1950s based on reverse-engineering of recovered alien spacecraft, and that the U.S. has a highly advanced secret space program. Most people in the UFO research community believe it is becoming increasingly difficult to distinguish our classified aircraft from alien craft. In *Mystery*, Keith reports there were often sightings of unmarked black helicopters in conjunction with the mutilations, suggesting human involvement, though perhaps just as observers.

There are many stories from military and other sources of an agreement made between someone or group in the Eisenhower administration and an extraterrestrial group, allowing human abduction in exchange for advanced technology. No documentation has yet been found and may never be found, but many within the UFO community suspect this story is true because of the credibility of the witnesses. As more people have felt safe to come forward with their abduction accounts, there does appear to have been an uptick in abductions in the later 1950s and 1960s. Cattle mutilations could possibly have been part of such a deal.

Linda Moulton Howe, one of the premier cattle mutilation and UFO researchers, believes that "negative" ETs are behind the mutilations of cattle and other animals, and that these negative ETS are a cause for concern. There are numerous accounts of the frequently reported "gray" aliens being associated with cattle mutilations, and Linda believes that reptilian types, often colluding with grays, may be the primary culprits. For a wealth of detailed reports on cattle mutilations, there are few better resources than Linda's earthfiles.com website and archives.

Pretty much all of the mutilation reports I've read report that the blood has been entirely drained from the carcasses. There are thousands of abduction witnesses that know they have been involved in hybrid breeding projects through the removal of ova and sperm. Given that blood is the perfect food for cell cultures, hybrid breeding projects are a potential explanation for cattle mutilations. Researcher Chuck Zukowski (ufonut.com) reported an apparent preference for organic or more naturally fed cattle, which could also be related to the use of blood for propagation of hybrids.

Another respected cattle mutilation researcher, Christopher O'Brien (*Stalking the Herd: Unraveling the Cattle Mutilation Mystery*) found that occurrences are commonly downwind from nuclear testing sites or nuclear plants, and he believes that whoever is doing them could be testing for radiation contamination or damage. Genitals and soft tissues around the mouth are routinely missing, which lends credence to this theory.

Along those lines, researcher John Rhodes looked at one hundred Montana cases and suggests a majority of cases occurred downwind from animal feedlots. There is a hog farm in the Dupuyer area that is upwind from where many cattle mutilations have occurred. Worldwide, we're seeing growing concern that hog farms, especially, are breeding grounds for Farm Animal MRSA (Methicillin Resistant Staphylococcus Aureus). MRSA is an extremely deadly form of bacteria that is highly resistant to antibiotic treatment due to overuse of antibiotics. It is often found in hospital settings and is responsible for many deaths. Rhodes wonders if whoever is doing the cattle mutilations is trying to tell us something. The tissues that are typically collected in these mutilations—lips, tongue, genitals—are where one would look to measure the effects of toxic exposure of one kind or another, so it's a theory worth considering. This kind of data could potentially be of interest and collected by humans or ETs. Rhodes' website is http://www.reptoids.com/Vault/mutebiohazard.htm.

As is the case with many mysteries in the field of Ufology, I doubt there is just one explanation. I think it likely that more than one thing could be occurring, but I do believe the evidence is compelling that many cases are ET related.

While the epoch of animal mutilation in the U.S. is generally thought to have started with Snippy the horse in Colorado in 1967, there are reports of this kind of mysterious phenomena going back hundreds of years (Chris O'Brien covers this well in *Stalking the Herd.*)

In Montana and much of the U.S, cattle mutilations became a widespread phenomenon in the 1970s. However, there is a 1947 case recorded by a Blackfeet tribal member from near Browning, Montana, part of Keith's study area, that I think is worth including in this republication of *Mystery Stalks the Prairie.*

Rod Skenandore, "Elk Chief," self-published his small book, *No More Secrets*, in 2001. I met Rod at an International UFO Conference, and because he was Blackfeet from Montana, I bought the book and spent some time talking with him. Later I connected with Rod to get more copies of the book for the Blackfeet College and Cultural Committee. He said the remainder of his books were irretrievable in

Oneida, Wisconsin, and that rather than making copies of the book I had, he wanted to rewrite the chapter with the cattle mutilation story. He sent his revision of the chapter "Twinkle Twinkle Little Star?" with added names and text, giving permission to copy and share it in 2016. Rod Skenandore died in August 2017, and his wife, Gudrun Roetzscher, granted permission to publish from his writings. The following is taken from his book and his 2016 revision:

* * *

Rod was eight years old in the summer of 1947, living at the Cut Bank Boarding School where his Blackfeet mother was an administrator. Early one morning, school friends Stenog and Chester yelled for Rod to come outside. He jumped out of bed, pulled on his cutoffs, and rushed outside. His friends took off and Rod ran after them to join a group of kids across the creek standing around a dead "white-face" cow.

Rod wrote, "Flies were spinning in and out of a perfectly round hole four inches across, cut into the side of the carcass, which also had the eyes, tongue and parts of its body removed."

Small stones thrown at the dead cow bounced off and rolled on the ground, leaving lines radiating out in the powdery dust.

"Many questions tempted us until Bull Calf, many called him Manny, strolled our way bearing a story, and my journey to the mysterious aspects of life, those rarely admitted, began."

Manny began: "A long time ago in the early 1900s, we used to watch lights come down to the ground a lot of the time. Sometimes they would be red, sometimes blue, green ones and yellow ones. Once I saw a bright white one that looked like it was going to crash .... The first time I went along with my relatives to learn what the lights were, we were surprised to see small men dressed in clothes that looked like metal but soft, moved like cloth. When they saw us, they just stood there not moving away, looking. Once an elder offered an eagle feather to one of them and he took it. They did not speak by using their mouth, but their messages came into our minds. We understood them that way."

At this point in the writing, Rod comments that Bull Calf was one of the last living elders that witnessed the coming of the White people. He spoke English but would rather speak the Blackfeet "Picuni" tongue and only used English for those who spoke no Indian. In his writing, Rod translates what Manny said that morning, and at later times, into his own words:

> "They told us they were relatives of ours and came down from a planet much like the Earth we lived on although there were some differences here they needed to know. They said they had been coming for many generations, living underground, and there were more like them but back then when there were less people and no guns, they came more. They liked Buffalo and Fish and had a way of catching them which worked with the Flying Boats we saw coming as lights."

Rod continues:

> "Bull Calf did not recall or wasn't sure of the location where the flying boat people came from but there were more than one planet and they did not live that far away, considering the vastness of space.

"Not only were there small people from sub-space localities here, tall men resided too. Some looked just like my own people with long black hair. Others had blond hair and shiny blue eyes. These tall beings could speak orally and used the same language the Indians did.... The tall ones were as though Chiefs and whenever they showed up, feasts were held in their honor. For these space-traveling entities to 'mix-in' with natives of that bygone era was not rare. In some aspects, we were the same.

"Joe Bull Calf, oldest son of Manny, had insights similar to his dad. When Joe would say things, it was as if he was relating something with the most confidential and personal intent. After Bull Calf made his knowledge available that day, Joe opened up with information of his experiences as well as some from what he had been told.... He thought they told him Buffalo were in existence on their ancient homeland as well.... The Blond-haired blue-eyed beings very ancient in lineage as well also had Cows on their planet.

"The little men also it seemed had a taste for Beef, and an eye witness account of another elder, a Crow Indian, whose name was "Bird In The Ground," ...from the south of Montana, related: Four little men, grey in color carrying a cow, each hoisting a leg, inside, to a round shaped craft shining brilliantly white which was concealed behind a grove of trees where it had landed and took off in a flash of light, after, they disappeared. As he stood there on his property watching and they came into view, he said they stopped and looking at him, acknowledged his presence. This was in the 50s."

Rod continues quoting Bull Calf's story as he remembers it:

"... many white lights were in the sky early this day. They were up on the ridge —which was a hill 1000 feet in elevation higher than where we stood around the cow's carcass—and I watched them land and take off to go into a bigger light higher up in the dark that looked just like the morning star hanging there glowing. Just before daybreak, they all left into the big light. I went up there and cows were laying all over the place and holes, just like this one here, were in them, none of them have any blood in them either."

Rod comments:

"Looking at the already mentioned lines fanning out from the underside of the dead cow's flattened body laying in the dust, puzzled me at first until Bull Calf explained he had seen this one being dropped from one of the lighted craft. Then it became clear, and I contemplated the rock I threw, which bounced off into the dust, make the same ray-like features.

"From what Bull Calf related, it erased questions that I had even then, in my inexperienced life; we were descendants in a particular way to those far traveled beings. We had come here in ages past, seeded to take care of the sacred Garden. Even the language we used was evidence of this and made the connection they enjoyed with the Spirit world a constant thing. The old ones, Bull Calf said, used few words to convey their intentions. They too, he related, were mentally gifted to the point that sign language fulfilled their conversations and that, coupled with the astute empathic abilities they possessed, was all they needed to carry out their roles as gardeners."

Rod relates additional information garnered from Bull Calf's stories at later times:

> "Of the beings who had come down visiting, citing kinships, they too lived on planets and considered their homes as Mother.... They were far more ancient in anatomical structure, that's all.... They never touted themselves as superior and never questioned the source of their onset. Basically, they gave thanks for every aspect of their journey just as did Bull Calf as well as all the others in those ancestral times.... Consequently, most of what has happened here on this our Earth, has transpired more than once in diverse galaxies across the vast expanse of the deep and watery space of time we call Universe.
>
> "Since then, of course and without any exception, I have strived to discover all I could about the importance of giving thanks for life no matter where it gathers or who seeded it originally.... Of all the versions I have encountered about how life came to be and how it was in the days of yore, I like what Bull Calf told me best."
>
> *—R.C. Skenandore—"Poun-Oh-Kah-Nay"—Elk Chief*

This story from the Blackfeet Reservation, adjacent to where Keith and his team did their investigations, offers a different perspective on the phenomenon of cattle mutilations. Though these stories came from a cattle mutilation event in 1947, and the teachings from elders and oral history it evoked, they are remarkably similar to what we are learning from modern-day witnesses about their ET encounters. In 2018, the results of a five-year study of human encounters with non-human intelligence (NHI) were published by the

Dr. Edgar Mitchell Foundation for Research into Extraterrestrial and Extraordinary Experiences (FREE). In their book, *Beyond UFOs: the Science of Consciousness and Contact with Non-Human Intelligence, Volume 1*, one of the most surprising results was that the overwhelming majority of individuals—66 percent—who encountered ETs viewed their experiences as mainly positive. Only five percent of the respondents viewed their experiences as mainly negative. The book summarizing the study is a treasure trove of information about the different kinds of ETs and the extraordinary experiences reported by the "contactees." One of their recurring themes is that many of the visitors explicitly say they are here to assist the people of Earth in a critical time, to help people achieve a higher level of consciousness and intelligent civilization.

Cattle mutilations are a disturbing phenomenon that have garnered a lot of attention in Montana and worldwide. For many people, especially rural folks, they have been an introduction to a possible alien presence on the planet. *Mystery Stalks the Prairie* was a seminal book in making people in Montana and beyond aware of the phenomena. Dispensing with mundane explanations, Keith Wolverton and his team were teased and ridiculed, yet they persevered in their dedicated efforts to solve the mystery and bring truth to light. They and their superior officers at the Cascade County Sheriff's office, John Krsul and then Glenn Osbourne, believed that the public deserved to know the results of their investigations, encouraged the research, and supported publication of the results. Given the suppression of information that was occurring at the time (and only recently is beginning to abate), it took great courage for all of those involved to get this book into print.

In the intervening years, so much more information has

come to light, along with a greater willingness to believe first-person accounts of contact. It's clear that some ETs do not have our best interests at heart, or are at least indifferent to human values and concerns. The UFO literature has plenty of accounts and warnings about negative ETs. Many believe these rogue ETs have been influencing affairs on Earth for a very long time, despite the "Prime Directive" ethic (often reported in ET literature and used in the *Star Trek* series) to not interfere in human affairs.

However, we are also learning that many and perhaps the majority of our visitors are benevolent; that they have been coming to Earth for a long time, and they may have seeded our planet from other, more advanced civilizations.

The stories related by Rod Skenandore and Manny Bull Calf of other inhabited planets and advanced subterranean Earth colonies are repeated in stories from other indigenous peoples around the world and in UFO and extraterrestrial circles and literature.

If, as so many are coming to believe, there are visitors who share our genetics and are benevolently concerned about our future, they could be important allies in overcoming the challenges we face. While these benevolent star people may have to abide by the Prime Directive ethic of non-interference, they can assist if asked, and apparently, they have been able to work with some individuals in dreams, "intuition," and sudden flashes of insight into problems.

We possess abundant evidence for a longstanding extraterrestrial presence on Earth. Examining it requires us to push through the intentional programming that deliberately casts doubt and discourages public interest in the subject. If we Earthlings as a whole can overcome our doubt and fear of extraterrestrial life, and believe the hopeful, inspiring reports from those who have had contact, the potential exists for growing, and perhaps resuming, relations with advanced, benevolent civilizations. Interplanetary partnerships and alliances could smooth our path to a brighter future. I sincerely hope such conscious relationships are part of our near future. May our hearts and minds be open.

Joan Bird
April, 2021

MYSTERY STALKS THE PRAIRIE

To JOHN C. KRSUL, Sheriff of Cascade County, Montana, and his staff, this book is dedicated with gratitude and appreciation.

Sheriff Krsul has realized, from the beginning, the importance of investigating reports of cattle mutilations, UFOs, hairy creatures and other phenomena. He has given his staff full support in their efforts to solve the mysterious happenings and his encouragement was important. In a very real sense, without Sheriff Krsul's help, this book would not have been written.

IN APPRECIATION

We are deeply grateful to the people who assisted, in various ways, with the investigations and thus helped to make this book possible.

A special tribute goes to those individuals who reported to law officers the strange incidents they witnessed. Without the co-operation of these conscientious citizens, there would have been no investigation.

We sincerely appreciate the contributions by physicians, veterinarians, pathologists, toxicologists, and others who shared their professional knowledge and skill.

Our thanks to the news media for the fine cooperation that made the task of investigation easier.

Most of all—we appreciate and want to thank those members of the Cascade County Sheriff's Department who shared and are still sharing the burden of investigation. They are Undersheriff Glenn Osborne, Deputies Ken Anderson, Arne Sand, and Shirley Peterson and Clerk Elaine Anderson.

Roberta Donovan and Keith Wolverton

ABOUT THE AUTHORS

Mystery Stalks the Prairie was written by two Montanans, Mrs. Roberta Donovan of Lewistown and Captain Keith Wolverton of Great Falls, a deputy sheriff for Cascade County.

Mrs. Donovan, a former newspaper reporter and editor, wrote this book and Captain Wolverton, an experienced lawman and the officer in charge of investigating reports of cattle mutilations, UFOs and hairy creatures, provided the information and technical advice.

This is the second book for Mrs. Donovan. Her fictionalized account of her father's boyhood in Montana's early days, *Ike—Boy of the Breaks*, was published in November, 1975, by T.H.A.R. Institute of Raynesford, Montana, the same firm publishing this book.

Mrs. Donovan is now an associate of T.H.A.R. Institute. Before joining the Institute's staff in March, 1976, she served for 12 years as editor of the *Lewistown (Mont.) News-Argus.*

She continues to do freelance writing for a number of publications, including some of national scope, and is a correspondent for the *Billings (Mont.) Gazette.*

Mrs. Donovan is a member and past president of Montana Press Women and in 1968 was named that organization's Montana Press Woman of the Year. She has won more than 100 state and national awards for her writing.

Mrs. Donovan is the mother of six grown children and has seven grandchildren.

Captain Wolverton, a native of Great Falls, has been a member of the Cascade County Sheriff's Department since 1965. He was one of two men responsible for establishing the Cascade County K-9 Academy, where lawmen and their

Roberta Donovan

Keith Wolverton

dogs are trained in a unique school. It is the only resident K-9 training academy in the United States. Captain Wolverton taught at the academy until 1975 when he was transferred to duty with the sheriff's office in Great Falls.

The events in this book represent countless hours of research and investigation on the part of Captain Wolverton and his fellow officers.

Over the years Captain Wolverton has attended a number of seminars and special schools to continue his specialized training as a law enforcement officer.

In 1972 the Great Falls Exchange Club selected Captain Wolverton as their Law Officer of the Year from all of the Great Falls, Cascade County and Malmstrom Air Force Base lawmen, as well as area members of the Montana Highway Patrol.

Captain Wolverton has been active in the Cascade County Sheriff's Posse which his father helped establish and has assisted in a number of rescues. He particularly enjoys participation in this organization because it is horse mounted. He is also a director of an Explorer Scout post.

Captain Wolverton is married and has two daughters and a son.

Editor's note: Roberta Donovan died in 2005. Keith Wolverton died in 2019.

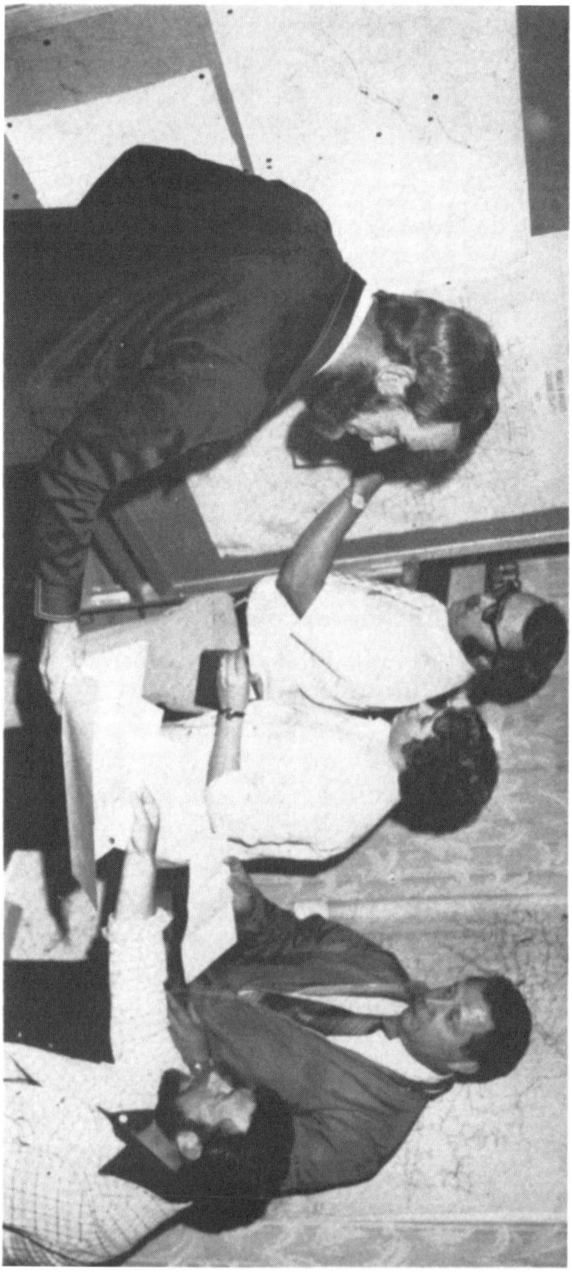

Members of the Cascade County Sheriff's Department team investigating cattle mutilations, sightings of unidentified flying objects, and the appearance of strange biped creatures look over some of the information they have assembled. They are (left to right) Deputy Ken Anderson, Undersheriff Glenn Osborne, Clerk Elaine Anderson, Deputy Arne Sand and Captain Keith Wolverton. Deputy Shirley Peterson was not present for the picture.

FOREWORD

We live in a strange and mysterious time.

Even though technological advances that boggle the mind with their intricacy are routine tools of scientists and a wealth of knowledge that includes the know-how to put an astronaut on the moon is at man's command; still, man is faced with some mysteries that defy solution.

Among these mysteries are the many cattle mutilations reported recently in north-central Montana. Investigating law officers are baffled by bizarre cases which seem to have no logical explanation. Diligent and intensive research by officers, assisted by pathologists, veterinarians, toxicologists and others, has failed to unravel the mystery.

Facts have been established, but the important question ... who is doing this and why ... has not been answered.

Some persons say the mutilations are caused by predators. This is occasionally true. However, it becomes difficult to blame a coyote or magpie predator when an investigator finds an exact round patch of hide has been neatly removed by a sharp instrument, or all of the blood has been removed from the animal, or the area around the animal appears burned, or all these incidents have occurred.

The puzzle becomes more obscure when, in most instances, no tracks—animal, human, or vehicle—are found. In other cases, investigators have found horse tracks in the mutilation area, but the landowner swore no horses had been there for many years.

This book relates some of these strange incidents, but it does not attempt to draw a conclusion. The events are factual, based on reports on file in the office of the Cascade

County (Montana) Sheriff's office. These reports are used with permission.

Other mysterious events which may or may not be related to the cattle mutilations are also reported here. These events include numerous reported sightings of unidentified flying objects (UFOs), unidentified helicopters and strange, hairy, man-like creatures.

Incidents reported here occurred between August, 1974, and May, 1976, in a five-county area of Montana which has had an appreciably large number of cattle mutilations.

Several stories and books are being written about cattle mutilations, UFOs, and hairy creatures. Some may be true. But there are others that investigation has proven to be false. Some writings are dramatized and sensationalized, perhaps to stimulate greater readership.

This is not our intention. As co-authors of *Mystery Stalks the Prairie*, we have been factual within the confines of our knowledge. And where there was a choice, we have chosen to underplay the situation, as there is no desire to create fear or panic.

We had two purposes in writing this book.

One is to let the American people know what is happening. We believe, but cannot prove, there are those who know what is behind these bizarre happenings, but for various reasons they are keeping silent. Others appear to ignore the situation, but it may be that they have not had access to certain facts, such as those uncovered by the Cascade County Sheriff's Department.

We believe the people have a right to know.

Our second reason for writing this book is there may be a chance, however slim, that this information may help solve the mystery and may bring new evidence to light. Mystery

Stalks the Prairie may also aid public officials to have a better understanding of what they are facing.

Except for those who are presently serving as law enforcement officers, all names of individuals have been omitted to protect them from implication in any way.

But the incidents are true—or as true as it is humanly possible to tell them.

Roberta Donovan, Keith Wolverton

CONTENTS

ILLUSTRATIONS

Chapter 1

Chapter 2

1

A CUT WITH A SERRATED EDGE

Who? Why?

From the beginning, these have been the two questions lawmen in a five-county area of north-central Montana have asked as they investigated one cattle mutilation after another.

Despite their best efforts, they have not yet found the answer.

Each baffling bit of evidence is scrutinized as they persist in their efforts to solve the mysteries and put an end to the bizarre incidents.

One of the most startling clues might have gone undetected if it had not been for the law officers' meticulous examination of the dead cow's carcass.

The Cascade County's Sheriff's Department had been called the afternoon of September 22, 1975, to investigate the death of two cows on a ranch near Belt, southeast of Great Falls. A veterinarian, who had seen the cows earlier, suspected mutilation and had advised the rancher to call the sheriff.

Initial examination of the first cow showed lawmen that the cow had obviously been mutilated. Dead about two days, the cow's bag, teats, rectal area and reproductive organs were removed, thus making it possible to look completely through the bag area and out the rectal opening.

What made this investigation different from those that had preceded it was the strange way the hide had been cut in removing the bag.

One of the deputies, in lifting some of the remaining hide, discovered that the cut, obviously made with a very sharp instrument, had serrated edges similar to those created with pinking shears. This was the first time the officers had encountered this type of cut.

Captain Keith Wolverton, Cascade County Sheriff's Deputy who had been working on mutilation cases for several months, decided to seek an expert opinion on the cut edge. A sample of the serrated hide was taken to a Montana medical pathologist, who confirmed the cut was made with a very sharp instrument. Captain Wolverton then took a sample to a well-known veterinary pathologist in Colorado and received the following report:

"This strip of skin had a long, straight cut edge with regular serrations (approximately 3/16 of an inch in width). Hair in one area had knowingly been clipped but in untouched areas the hair had been cut at the laceration edge. Changes on the skin edge resembled neither tooth marks of a predator, nor those of wire lacerations. The changes were similar to those that could be made by a knife except the regular striations."

The pathologist's reports were of primary importance to the small team of law officers investigating such incidents because the reports directly challenged the theory frequently advanced by some people who said mutilations did not occur but the severance of tissue from a carcass was the work of predators.

Coyotes may feast upon a carcass, but they do not leave a neatly serrated edge where they gnaw away the hide!

Colored photographs of the carcass, taken by Deputy Ken Anderson, provide additional evidence that the hide cut had a precise serrated edge.

The serrated cut discovery was considered a major break-

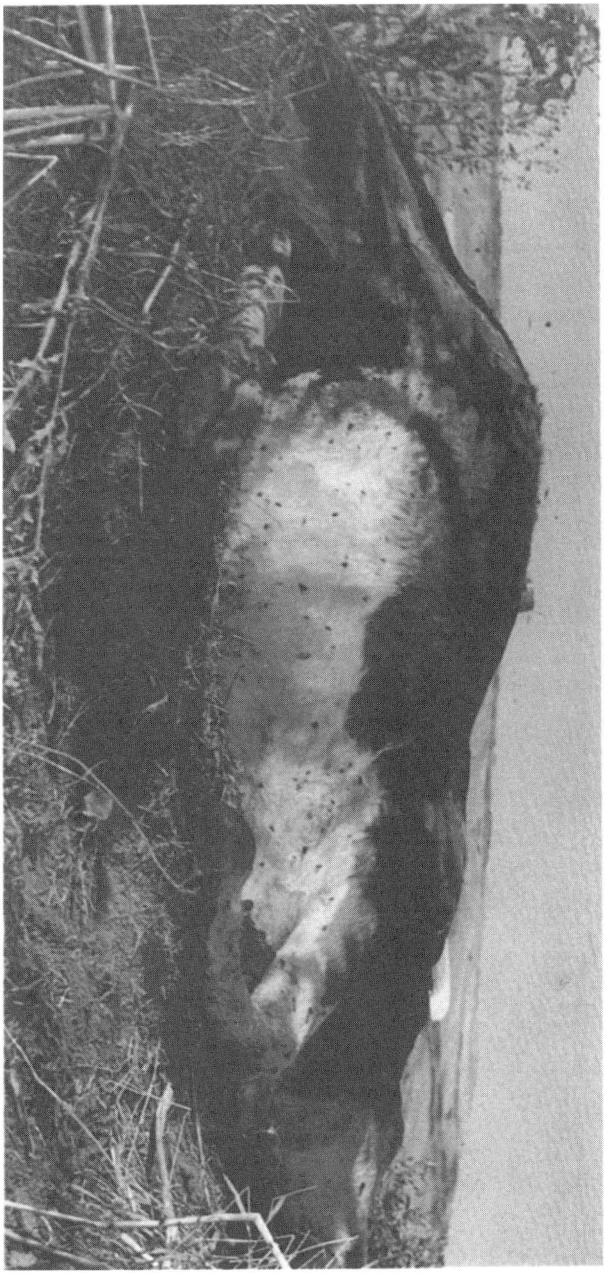

This photograph and the closeup of the cut (following page) show the way this cow's hide was cut, leaving an evenly serrated edge. The report of an animal pathologist ruled out any possibility of the cut being done by a predator. Lawmen have not been able to determine what type of instrument may have been used to make the cut.

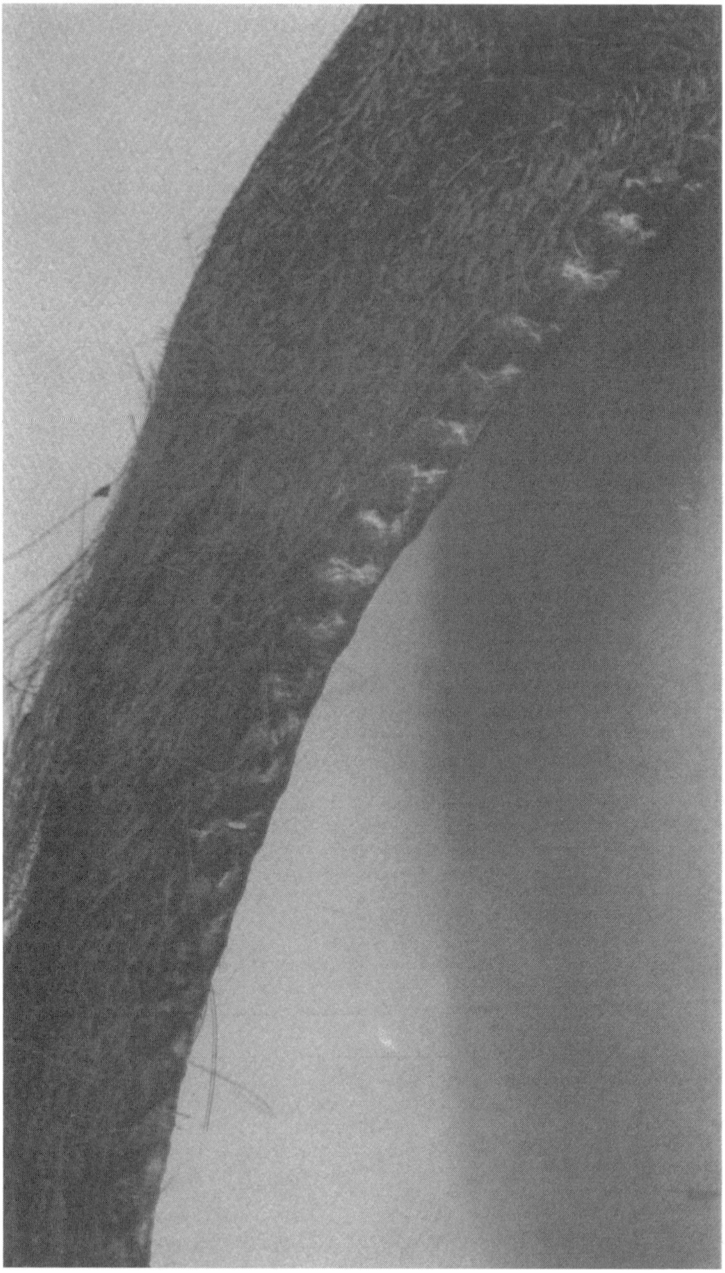

through in a sometimes frustrating and often perplexing investigation. Reports of possible cattle mutilations had been received in the Cascade County Sheriff's Office since August, 1974, but the number of such incidents began to markedly increase during the late summer and early fall of the following year. Although some mutilations were attributed to predators, it was obvious in other cases something else had occurred.

But what?

Each report was extensively investigated and bits of evidence were assembled, studied, analyzed. It was obvious that the cattle were dead. However, in many instances it was equally discernible that the cattle were mutilated.

The question of who or what is causing mutilations continues unanswered today.

Many theories have been advanced. Some of them are proclaimed by concerned and reliable citizens who believe a wide spectrum of possibilities from Satan cults to flying saucers. However, these associations have not been proven.

After almost a year of intensive investigation, Captain Wolverton remarked, "I'm no longer as eager to find out who is doing it as I am to discover why!"

Like working on a giant jigsaw puzzle, law officers have pieced together bits and scraps of information, but they are not always certain that they have a connection with the complete picture. The officers always thoroughly investigate the entire episode.

An important puzzle segment was found just 24 days after the serrated cut was discovered.

On October 16, 1975, the sheriff's department was called to investigate the death of another cow in the Belt area. The perplexity of the situation was increased by the fact the dead cow was found in a securely locked pasture and there were no visible tracks in the area.

The absence of tracks has consistently been one of the most baffling aspects of the cattle mutilations in Montana. The few tracks that have been found around mutilations were those of other cattle. The absence of tracks is unusual because the ground around the dead cows was often soft, muddy or covered with snow.

Examination of this cow showed that its left jaw had been skinned, its tongue excised and the right eye removed, not from the socket, but through the bone directly above the eye.

A significant discovery was made by the veterinarian who removed certain organs and other parts of the carcass for a toxicology examination. In skinning the animal, the veterinarian found what appeared to be a needle mark on the upper left leg. The mark went through the hide and into the flesh.

Did this indicate that the animal was injected with a drug to either anesthetize or kill it before the mutilation took place?

The tissue around the mark was removed for examination, along with the heart, liver, lungs, skeletal tissue, and bladder. In addition, the cuts around the head and eye were removed for analyses.

No drug was positively identified in analyses, but laboratory examination identified another unique clue. Cut areas on the jaw and around the eye not only had a serrated edge, but were burned.

Immediately after the first discovery of a serrated cut, officers tried to duplicate the cuts with various instruments, including a pizza cutter, leather stitcher and pinking scissors. The results were similar, but not identical.

Perhaps, the lawmen jested, whoever or whatever was do-

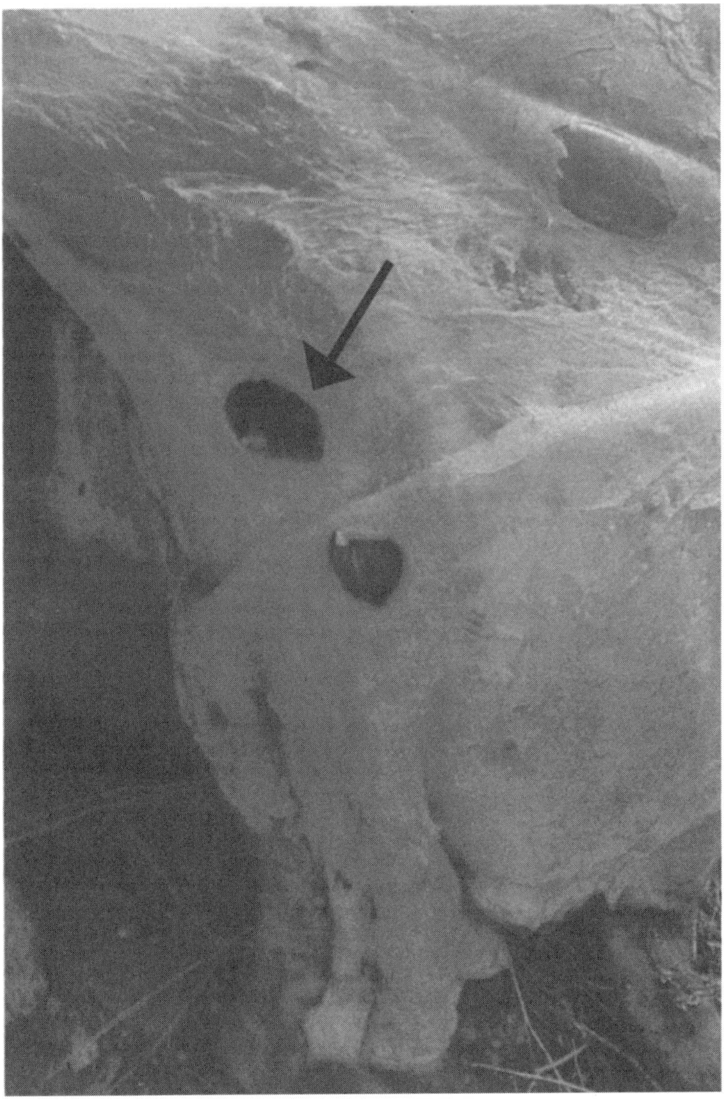

In skinning a mutilated cow, a veterinarian discovered what appeared to be a needle puncture wound in the upper left leg. The photo shows the wound (arrow) after the area around it was removed for analyses. Lawmen pondered whether the wound meant the cow had been injected with a drug to either anesthetize or kill it before mutilation.

Another clue to the mystery was added when a section of this cut area on the jaw was examined at a laboratory. It showed that the cut not only had a serrated edge, but that it had also definitely been burned.

ing the mutilations had a giant cooky cutter that made the serrated cuts!

After discovery of the burned and serrated cut, officers learned from a visitor to their office, who had had experience with laser beams, that this type of edge could be produced in metal using lasers. As yet it has not been possible to determine if serration can be produced on cowhide with laser.

Another mystifying bit of evidence surfaced when Undersheriff Jerry Skelton of Judith Basin County investigated a calf mutilation near Utica.

Undersheriff Skelton was called October 9, 1975, to investigate the death of the bull calf. Its testicles had been removed, as well as the cords leading to them. The only evidence he found at the scene—and it seemed to have no logical explanation—was that several stones, weighing as much as six or seven pounds each, were moved from a nearby rock pile. The rocks were turned over and moved around.

Undersheriff Skelton removed some parts of the calf for examination by a toxicologist and left the carcass at the place where he found it.

Ten days later, at the request of the rancher who owned the calf, Undersheriff Skelton returned to the scene.

During the ten days since the first investigation a snow had fallen in the area and later melted. The calf was found covered with a filmy white substance that stretched from the carcass to the surrounding ground like a cobweb. Laboratory tests identified it as petroleum distillate.

No one seems to know why the calf was shrouded in the substance.

But perhaps the most unusual incident investigated so far has involved not cattle, but a Shetland pony.

It took place in Teton County northwest of Great Falls

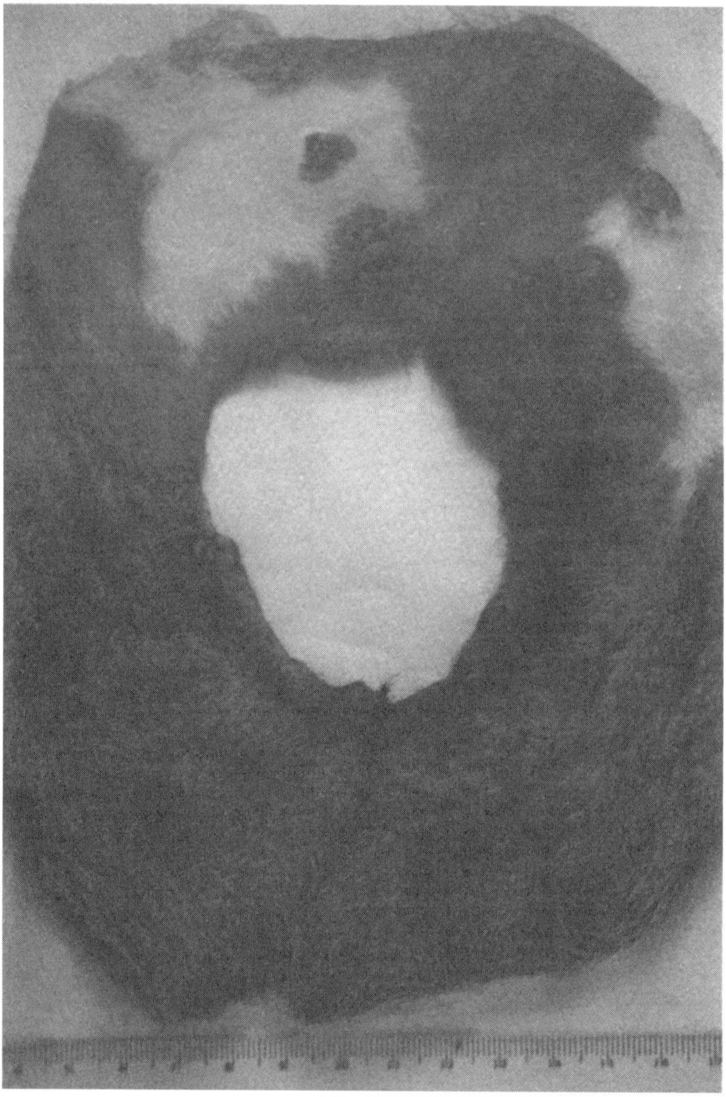

Part of its male organs were removed from a calf through this incision. The mutilation took place in Judith Basin County.

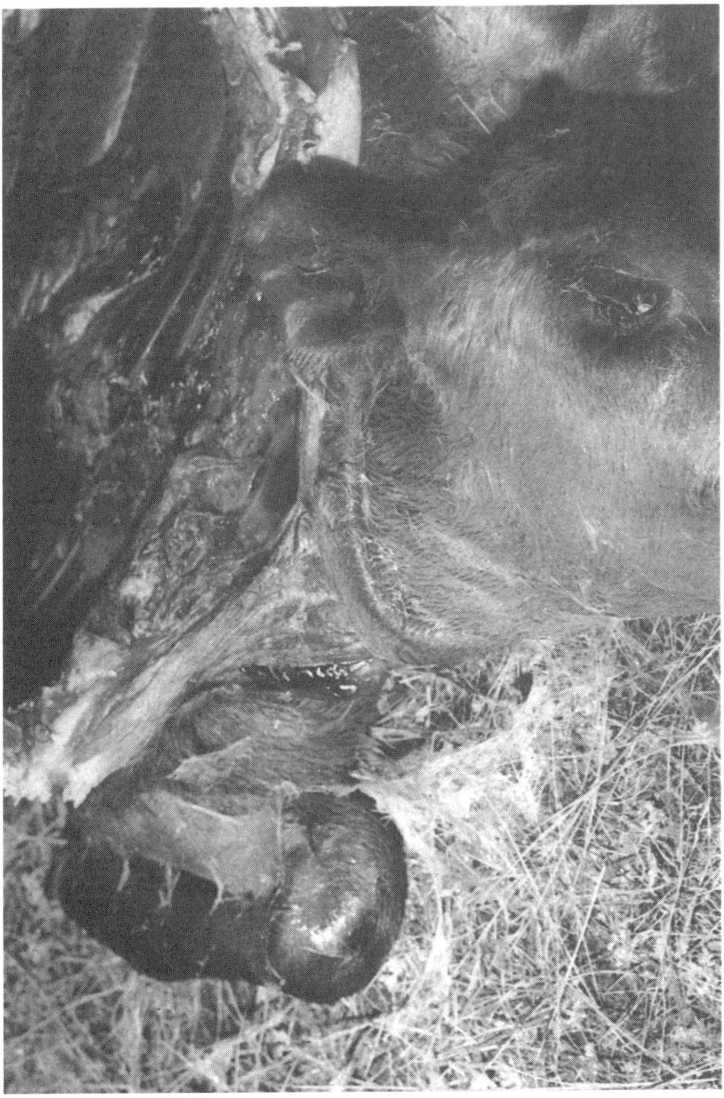

This is the same calf as on the preceding page, in a photo taken ten days later. It shows the white residue which stretched from the calf to the ground like a cobweb. The substance proved to be a petroleum distillate.

and Pete Howard, the Sheriff, asked the assistance of the Cascade County Sheriff's Office in investigating the possible mutilation.

Captain Keith Wolverton and Deputy Arne Sand responded. The Cascade County officers and Sheriff Howard were joined by a veterinarian and two livestock inspectors. They found the Shetland stud lying on its left side. All of its male organs had been removed and it was evident a very sharp instrument had been used in the tissue removal.

When the veterinarian, in the course of his examination, opened the horse's throat, he discovered two puncture wounds with corresponding bruises.

The most surprising development came when the veterinarian cut open the horse's body and found that it contained no blood except for a minute amount which he collected in two small vials.

Since the horse had weighed about 600 pounds, the veterinarian estimated the horse should have about 60 pounds (or 60 pints) of blood. He suggested that removal of this quantity of blood with hand-operated equipment would require a minimum of 90 minutes. A battery-operated pump devise would have reduced the time to approximately 15 minutes.

In subsequent cattle investigations wherein all of the blood was removed, an animal pathologist stated that it is usually impossible to remove all of the blood because when a third of the blood is removed the veins collapse.

However, it could be done, he stated, by injecting a saline solution into the heart (while the animal is alive) to increase the heart action and pump the blood faster. He added that it is next to impossible to detect the saline solution during autopsy.

The Shetland pony was seen by its owner's neighbor about

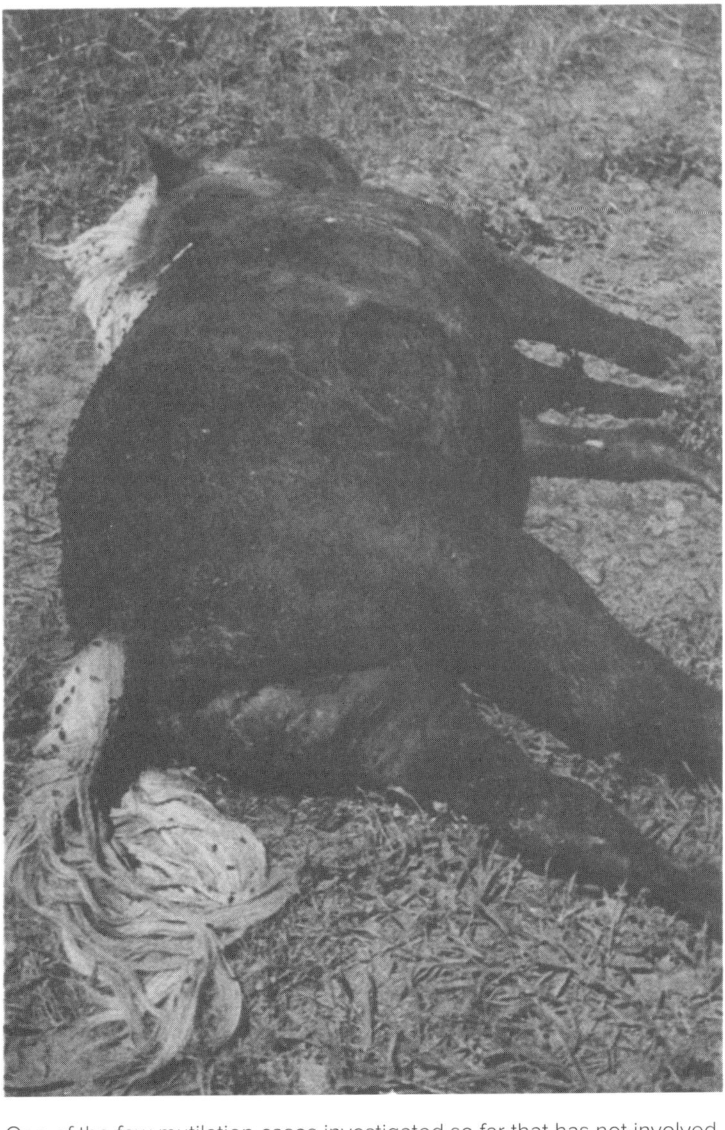

One of the few mutilation cases investigated so far that has not involved cattle is this Shetland pony which was killed in Teton County. All of its male organs had been removed with a sharp instrument and the carcass was completely void of blood. A pathologist stated that it is impossible to remove all of the blood because by the time a third of it is removed, the veins collapse.

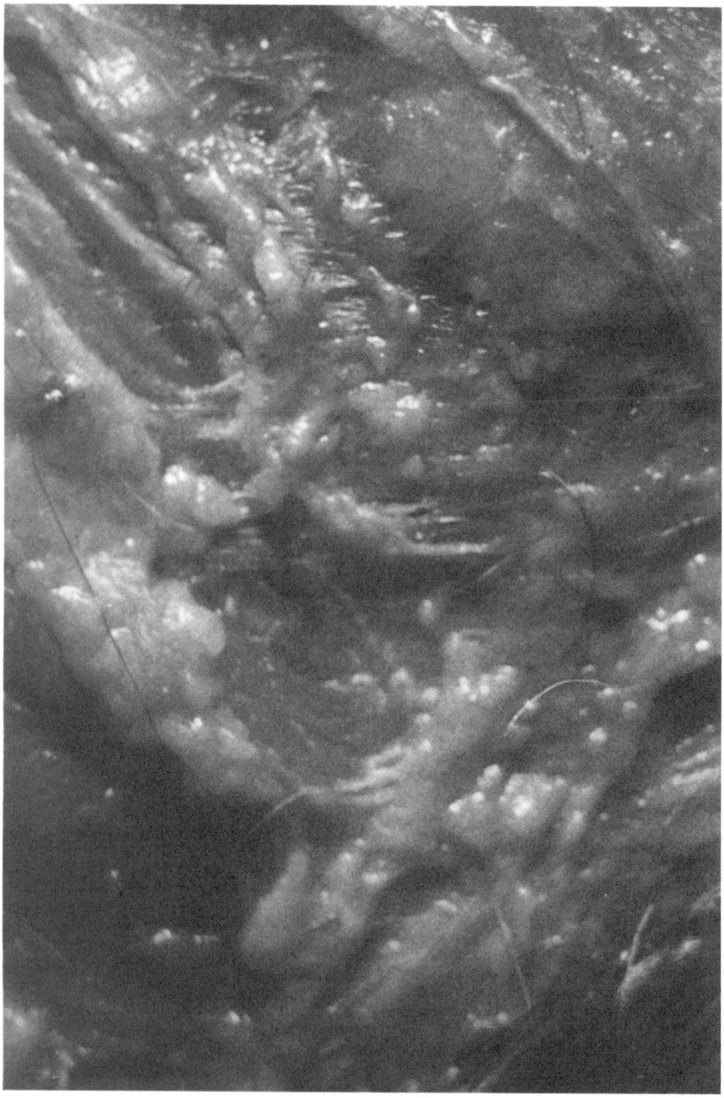

Close examination of the Shetland pony (see preceding page) by a veterinarian disclosed two puncture wounds in the throat. Similar puncture marks were found later in the jugular veins of other mutilated animals and in each instance the two wounds were the same distance apart.

three or four days before its carcass was found. The neighbor told officers he saw the small horse lying on the bank above an irrigation ditch and thought it looked sick or dead, so he yelled at it. When it raised its head, the neighbor assumed it was all right and went on. Later the same evening he saw the horse lying on the pasture side of the irrigation dike, where its carcass was found, but the neighbor was busy irrigating, and he did not stop to investigate.

The veterinarian was unable to determine the cause of the animal's death. Puncture throat wounds suggested the injection of drugs or another substance to tranquilize or kill the Shetland pony.

Through investigation it was established that the Shetland pony was mutilated during daylight hours and yet no one saw it happen or even saw anything unusual in the area.

To determine the exact time of mutilations has not been possible, but it is believed most of them occur at night.

Even though many mutilations are reported in Montana, not one person has ever reported seeing one take place.

2

CASE OF THE MISSING CALF

Evidence gained in investigating a number of mutilations, including the Shetland pony, seemed to indicate that the animals were tranquilized or anesthetized (but not killed) before they were mutilated. A veterinarian's theory that the drug Ketaset, could have been used for this purpose greatly interested investigating officers.

The lawmen decided to perform an experiment to observe the effects of Ketaset on a calf. A Teton County rancher, who was interested in seeing the mutilations solved, offered to donate a crippled steer calf for the experiment.

A veterinarian conducted the experiment with lawmen from both Teton and Cascade Counties observing.

The 250-pound calf was initially injected with 5 cc of Ketaset. Seven and a half minutes later the calf still appeared normal, so another 10 cc of Ketaset was injected.

Within three and a half minutes the calf was down on the ground. By the time four minutes had passed, the calf s heartbeat had increased from 60 to 120 beats per minute. During the rapid heartbeat, the veterinarian inserted a 12-gauge needle in the calf's jugular vein and the blood pumped out rapidly and regularly.

The calf s heartbeat slowed to 90 within 12½ minutes and after 21 minutes had passed, the calf was on its feet. Twenty-eight and a half minutes after injection of Ketaset, the calf was no longer under the influence of the drug. The calf was later returned to its owner.

Those witnessing the experiment agreed that during the period of time when the calf was rendered unconscious by the drug, it was unable to resist anything that was done to it.

The experiment proved that Ketaset could be used to quickly render an animal helpless and that it increased the heartbeat, which reduced the time needed to remove the animal's blood.

The experiment was but a part of the intensive efforts being made by law officers all over north-central Montana to solve the mysterious mutilations. With the advent of August, the number of mutilations increased considerably and at times the officers were hard-pressed to follow up on all reports.

Pete Howard, Sheriff of Teton County, may have set some sort of record when he investigated reports of three mutilations in one night.

The first report involved a 12-day-old heifer calf that had appeared to be in good health two days earlier when seen by the rancher. The calf was found in an isolated area, lying on a grassy hillside about 50 yards from a stock pond. Sheriff Howard commented on the fact that there seemed to be water nearby in most mutilation cases.

This particular incident was one of the few in which tracks were found in the area. A set of visible tire tracks in the grass indicated a vehicle had come down from the top of the hill, stopped on a small bench above the calf, and had later turned around and gone back up the hill.

However, there were no tracks visible in the immediate area of the calf s carcass.

There was no indication of a struggle and the investigating officers were unable to find any blood in the area. When the postmortem was done by a local veterinarian, he found the body cavity almost completely void of blood. Even the heart had very little blood in it.

The vulva and rectum had been removed from the body, along with a piece of hide about one foot in diameter. Also missing were some of the internal organs, including the bladder.

Although the mother cow was in the area when lawmen arrived, she made no effort to go near the dead calf, nor would other cattle in the herd go near it.

After delivering the calf carcass to the veterinarian for autopsy, Sheriff Howard asked Cascade County Deputies, Captain Keith Wolverton, Ken Anderson, and Arne Sand, to join him and assist with the investigation of the other two mutilated calves.

These two dead calves had been reported by a Fairfield area rancher. The area where they were found was quite remote, with no houses nearby. As in the previous case, there was a pond of water near.

It appeared that one of the calves had dropped into the water and had been dragged back away from the water about 12 or 14 feet. The sheriff's report stated: "It appeared that possibly two people had dragged the animal as there were no hesitation marks in the skid path as would likely be present if one person had dragged it."

This calf was a Black Angus heifer about four months old. It was missing the tip of its left ear, the vaginal and rectal areas had been removed, and the tail. As has been noted in a number of mutilations, the animal's eyes protruded extensively.

The second calf, a five-month-old Hereford heifer, had a large diagonal incision under the left rib section, near the flank. The intestines were protruding from the wound, through which the female reproductive organs had been removed. Again, the tip of the left ear was missing.

The incision in the calf s side was the kind usually made when performing a Caesarian on a cow to deliver a calf, giving further credibility to the theory that whoever was doing the mutilations was familiar with anatomy and surgical procedures.

The carcasses of the two calves were found about 12 feet apart.

The owner said when he first viewed the dead calves he noted that the herd from which they came was watering at the pond, but in an area they normally did not use. He said the cattle appeared to be quite listless.

Shortly after the officers arrived, the cattle spooked and ran off.

A neighbor reported seeing a car drive through the herd a few nights earlier. Officers speculated on the possibility the animals were selected before mutilation.

Just one week after officers investigated the three calf mutilations in Teton County, the Cascade County Sheriff's Office received two calls one day and another on the ensuing day regarding cattle mutilations in their county. Each of the three incidents had unusual circumstances not encountered earlier and these added to the mystery.

A unique mutilation method was revealed in an investigation north of Cascade involving a bull calf.

The rancher found the dead calf while checking cattle on top of a high butte. The calf was lying on its left side, about 40 feet from a stock tank. Again, water was near the mutilation site.

The right hind leg of the calf had been removed in a cir-

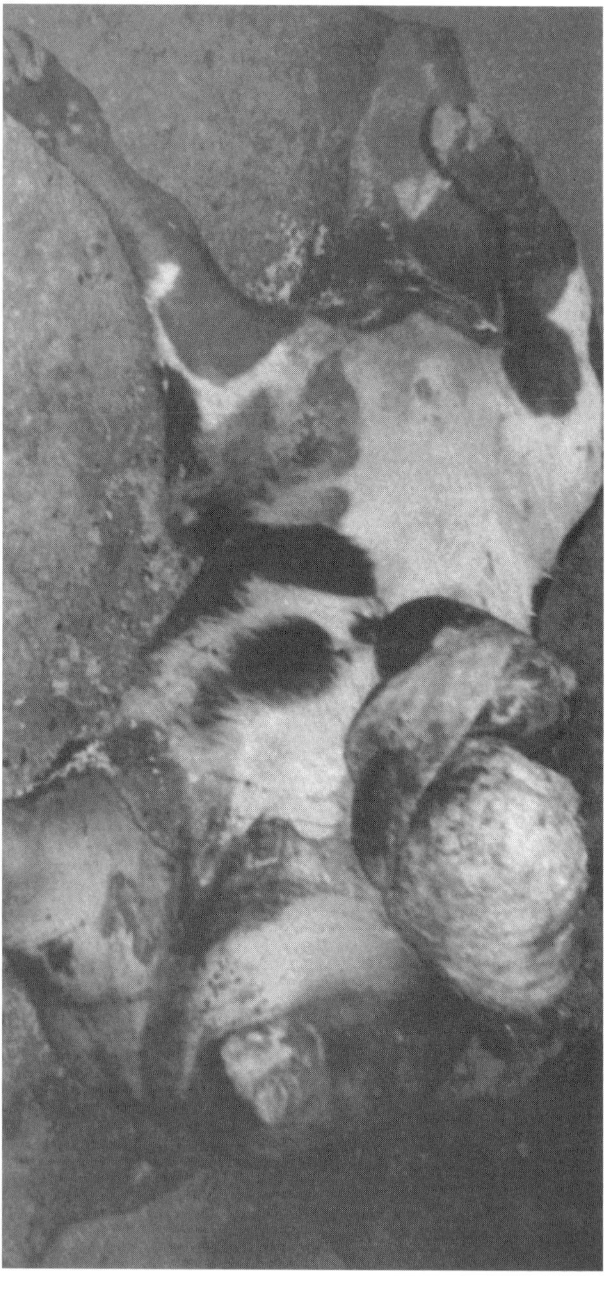

The incision in the side of this mutilated calf is the type used in performing caesarians on cows, causing lawmen to consider the possibility that those doing the mutilations were familiar with anatomy and surgical procedures. The calf's female organs had been removed and the intestines were protruding from the wound.

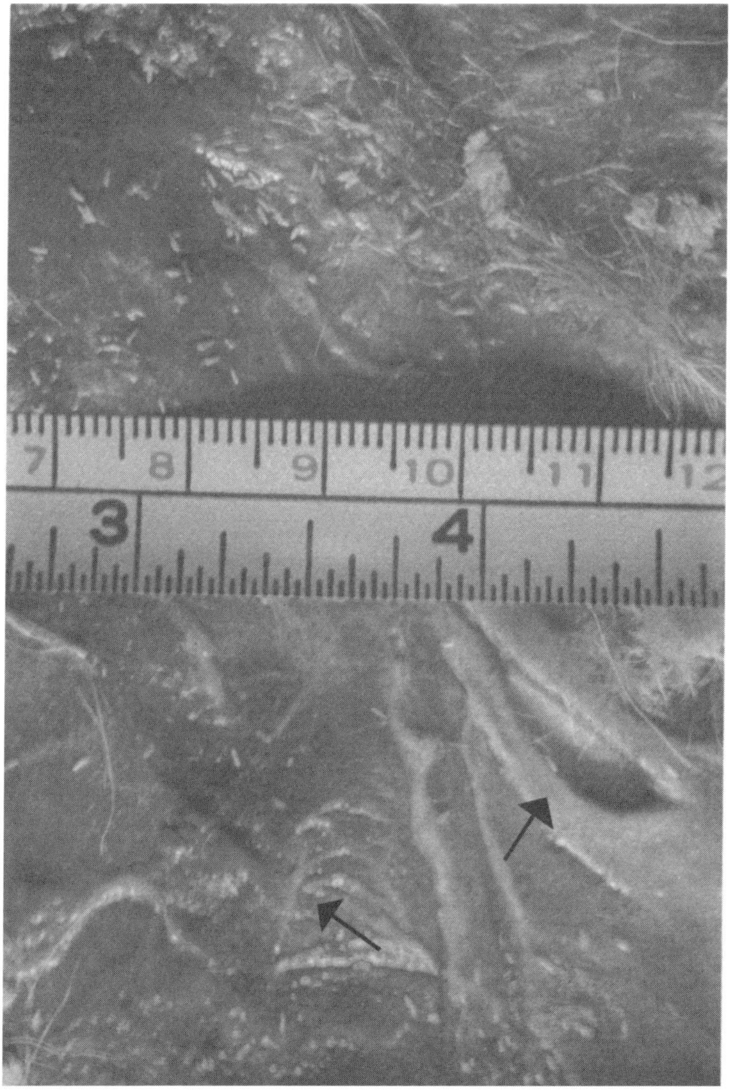

Puncture wounds like these in the jugular vein of the animal have been found in a number of mutilation cases. The theory has been advanced that a salt solution (to facilitate blood removal) was injected in the one opening while the blood was pumped from the other.

This is Square Butte, north of Cascade, where a mutilated calf was found on top of the butte. The area would have to be reached either by a county road, or by climbing a drainage that went from a pipeline at the top of the butte to a pump-house 600 feet below. Although the area was carefully searched, no footprints or tire tracks were found.

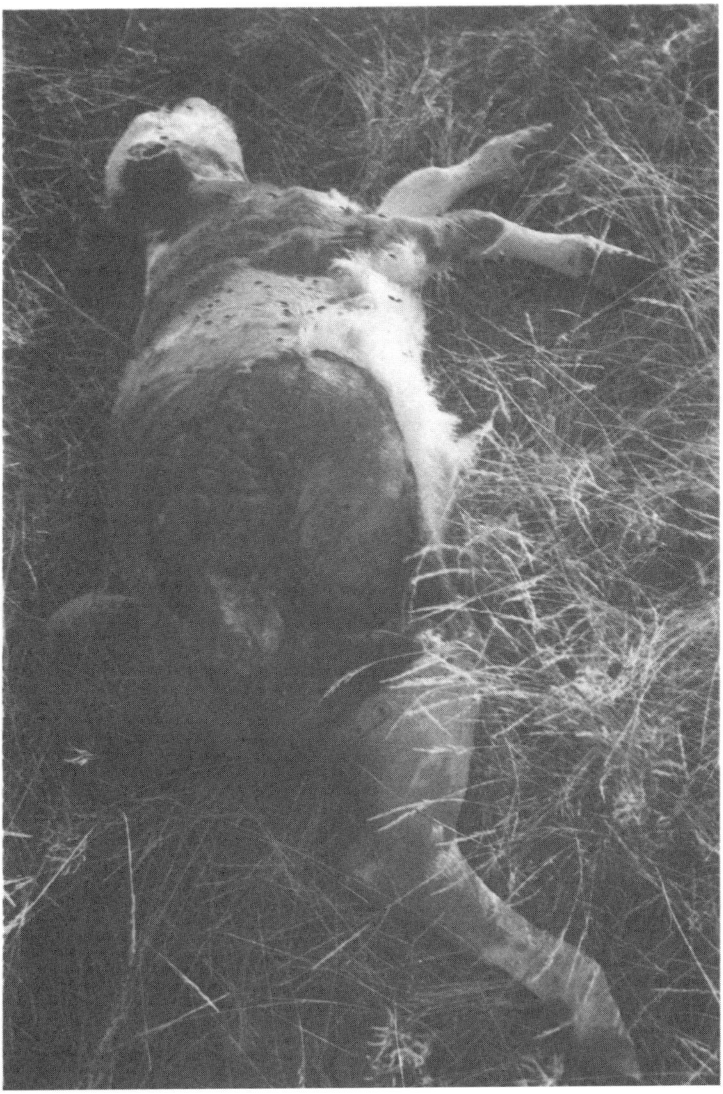

Lawmen encountered something different when they examined this mutilated calf, as the hind leg had been removed in a cut that went through the bone, as well as the flesh, just below the hip socket. Even though the bone was severed, there was no bone dust.

cular cut that appeared to be made with a sharp instrument. The cut went completely through the leg bone just below the hip socket. Even though the bone was severed, investigating officers could find no trace of bone dust.

The circular cut extended toward the midsection, exposing the stomach area. All of the sex organs had been removed, including the testicles, but the empty scrotum was still intact.

In turning over the calf, officers found one of its internal organs mashed beneath its left front quarter. Officers agreed the organ had to have been removed first, placed on the ground and the calf turned over on top of it.

Although the entire area was checked, no footprints or other evidence were found. Five nights earlier, a car had been observed at 7:30 and at 11:50 p.m. on the approach from the main county road. The top of the butte may also be reached by climbing a pipeline drainage from a pumphouse 600 feet below to the top of the butte.

The absence of tracks baffled officers when they investigated another reported mutilation the same week, near Belt. Few tracks have ever been found at mutilation sites, but this time it was an even greater mystery because the dead cow was found in a plowed field.

A theory had been advanced earlier that whoever was mutilating stood on a sheet of cardboard to avoid leaving tracks. However, in this case, the use of cardboard, as well as footprints or vehicle tracks, would have pressed down the furrows of loose soil. The cow was found three-quarters of a mile from the fence line and road.

When the rancher first found his cow, he noticed that one ear was missing. After dragging her out of the field, he noticed that the two teats on the right side had been cut off and

When officers turned over the dead calf, they found that one of the calf's organs had been removed and the calf laid on top of it, smashing it.

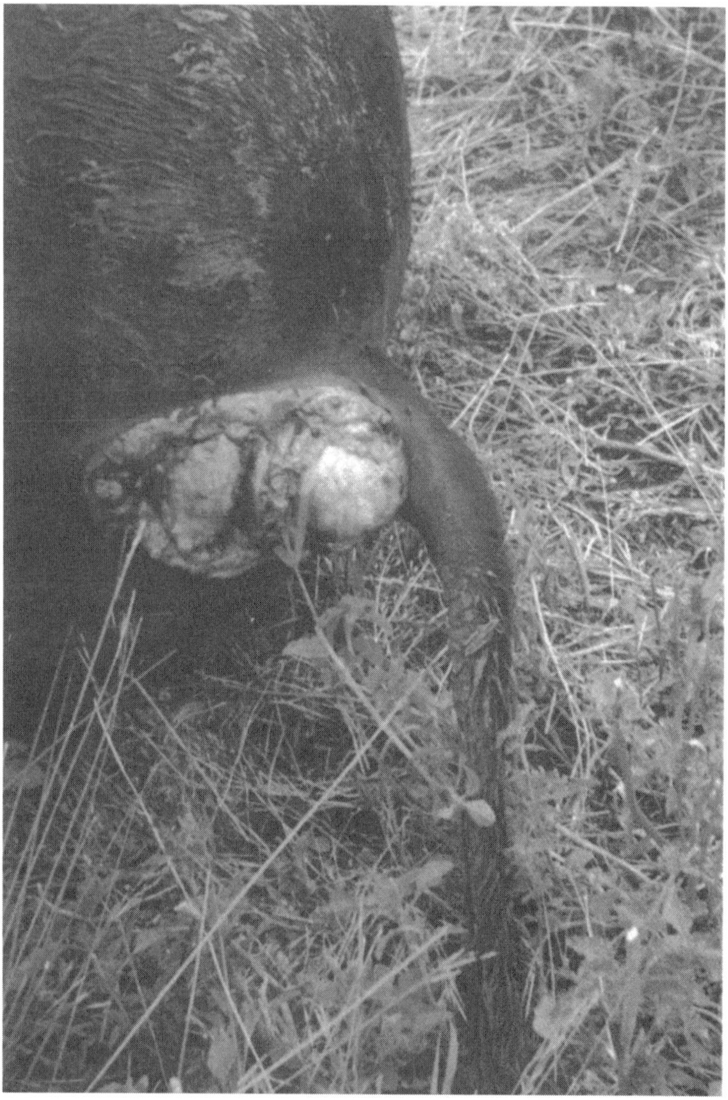

This mutilated cow was found in a plowed field, three quarters of a mile from the fence line, but there were no tracks in the area. The rectal area had been removed.

This wound underneath the front leg in the mutilated cow (previous photo) did not hold special significance at the time of the investigation. Months later some deputies from Idaho remarked that they had found a similar wound in a mutilated cow in their area, and a veterinarian had discovered the wound went all the way to the heart.

the rectal area removed, obviously with a very sharp instrument. It was at this point he called the Sheriff's Office.

Later examination showed that the cow had an incision underneath the front leg. Sgt. Les Bobier, one of the investigating deputies, cleaned the area and opened the wound, but no special significance was given to it until months later when some deputies from Idaho were visiting the Cascade County Sheriff's Department.

In looking at the department's photos of mutilations, one of the Idaho deputies remarked about this cow's incision. He said there had been a similar wound in a mutilated cow his department had examined. They had called in a veterinarian to do an autopsy and the veterinarian inserted an instrument into the wound and discovered that the opening went all the way to the heart.

Was this another piece of the complicated puzzle?

Another mutilation report was received the same day—August 14,1975—from another rancher in the Belt area. Incidentally, this date was the exact first anniversary of the first mutilation report received by the Cascade County Sheriff's Office.

A writer of "who done it" stories might have dubbed this incident, "The Mystery of the Missing Calf."

In this instance, the rancher found his mutilated Hereford cow in a locked pasture, about one-half mile from the county road. Her calf, born earlier in the spring, was missing. Lawmen were unable to find any tracks except those made by the cattle.

At the time of this writing, the calf has not been found.

This cow mutilation differed from the other cases because the reproductive organs and teats were not removed. The cow's left ear, tongue and some hide were missing. There was an attempt to skin the jaw. Examination showed that the gland behind the left ear had been removed.

The fact that there were no tracks puzzled the officers. The gate to the pasture was locked and anyone wanting to reach the cow would have had to walk about a half mile from the county road after crossing the fence; unless a helicopter or some other air or space vehicle was used—a theory which has been considered.

Although this was Cascade County's first case in which a calf was missing, Chouteau County had one similar incident. It was reported earlier in the year, on March 24, and was investigated by Deputy Robert Blades, another deputy and a livestock inspector.

It was necessary for the rancher to take the officers to the scene in a four-wheel-drive vehicle because of muddy conditions near the Missouri River.

The rancher told officers he had discovered one of his cows was missing that morning and that the rest of the cattle seemed to be very nervous and jumpy.

A large heifer cow was found lying at the bottom of a coulee. Deputies could find no human footprints in the area nor could they find any vehicle tracks, except those made by the rancher.

There was blood and signs of a scuffle in a circle about ten yards wide around the carcass.

The mutilation had apparently taken place only a short time before, as the carcass was still warm and steaming where the blood was draining out.

The udder bag was removed by a very smooth incision and the cow's intestines and internal organs were hanging out from the rectal area.

Dog or coyote tracks were found about 20 yards and farther from the carcass, but not closer.

In searching the area, the officers came across a newborn

calf that had been mutilated but was still alive. Its tongue and one lip had been removed. The mutilated calf did not belong to the mutilated heifer, according to the rancher's records, but the mutilated heifer's calf, born two days earlier, was missing and it had a white face. The mutilated calf was brown.

The entire area was searched for the missing calf, but it was not found. However, four days later, it mysteriously reappeared in the same pasture, lying on a snowbank. It was barely alive, but had not been mutilated.

The rancher later told authorities that four of his calves were born dead following the incident, although his cows had not had stillborns before. He said he put the four stillborn calves in a ravine, and they were immediately eaten by predators. However, the mutilated cow and calf were not touched by predators and finally deteriorated due to the elements.

Another unusual aspect of the case surfaced when tracks resembling those made by a horse were found in one part of the fenced pasture, but the rancher stated there had been no horses in the pasture for 20 years.

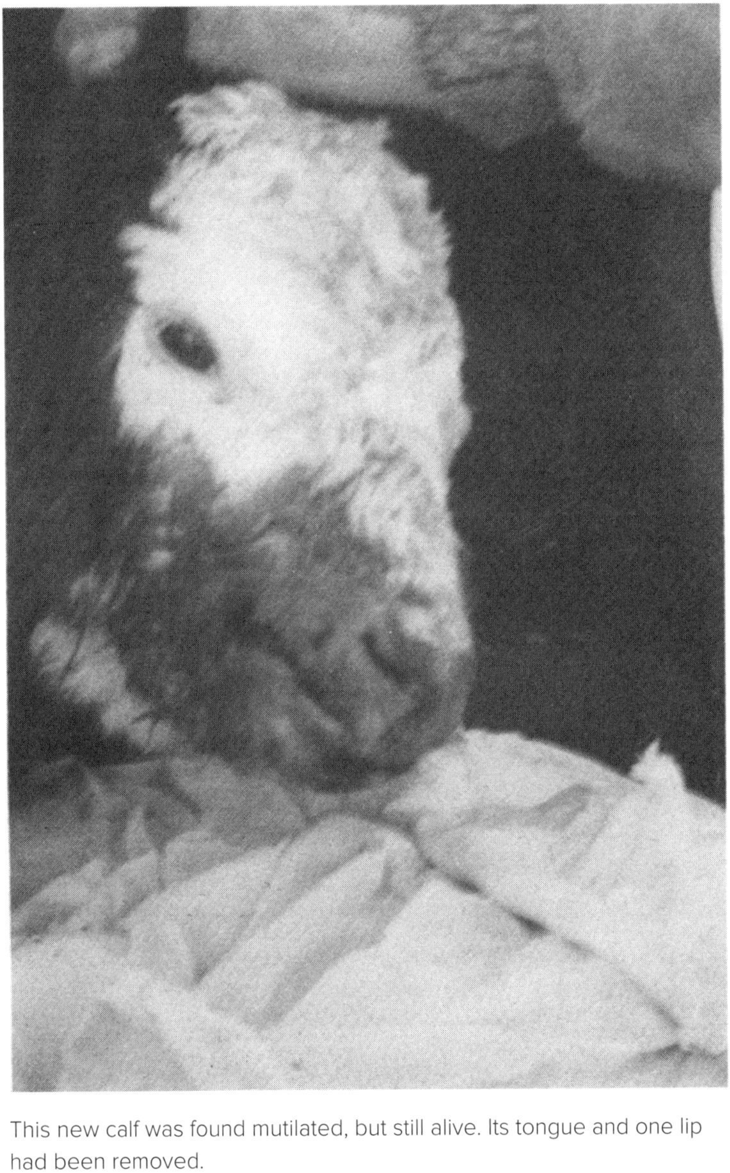

This new calf was found mutilated, but still alive. Its tongue and one lip had been removed.

3

APPEAL MADE FOR PUBLIC'S HELP

The first cattle mutilation reported to the Cascade County Sheriff's Department was on August 14, 1974. While there continued to be isolated incidents in the weeks and months that followed, it was the following summer when the number of mutilations started increasing at an alarming rate.

But apparently whoever or whatever was responsible for the mutilations was just beginning, as during the period from Aug. 1975, to May 1976, over 100 possible mutilations were reported to the Cascade County Sheriff's Department.

The bulk of the incidents occurred during warm weather, particularly in August and September. Records of investigations revealed that most of the mutilations took place at the time of the full moon. Whether this has any special significance, other than the fact the moon would provide light for the task, has not been established. If, as some people believe, some cult is responsible for the mutilations, it is possible the moon's phase could have a bearing on it.

It is difficult to determine the exact number of mutilations. Some of the incidents appear to be the work of predators and in other cases the animal has been dead too long to accurately determine what has happened.

On the other hand, it is safe to assume that there are a number of other incidents not reported, either because of fear or because the rancher assumed the animal was killed by predators.

In many cases, the exact cause of death has not been established. Although it appears that mutilations take place before death, there are some cases, according to pathologists and veterinarians, that cattle apparently died of natural causes and were mutilated after death.

The mysterious episodes drew the interest of Captain Keith Wolverton, a deputy with ten years of experience in the Cascade County Sheriff's Department. He had transferred to the Sheriff's Great Falls office in May, 1975, after serving at the Cascade County K-9 Academy southeast of Great Falls, a training school for law enforcement dogs which he helped establish.

When the mutilation reports began increasing, Captain Wolverton asked permission of his boss, Sheriff John Krsul, to devote three weeks of his time trying to solve them.

"I thought I could solve them in that time," Captain Wolverton said, "but the time went by and I hadn't solved anything. There's no school to train you in this kind of investigation. So far, I have just been trying to get the facts together, but I haven't solved it yet, so I must be missing some information."

What started out to be three weeks of investigation has continued for almost a year, with the full support of Sheriff Krsul. At times Captain Wolverton and the men working with him have become discouraged. But, since Sheriff Krsul considers the mutilations a law enforcement problem, the investigation continues.

Every lead has been researched, every report investigated, but many incidents have yielded no new clues.

Innumerable hours, particularly at night, have been spent by Captain Wolverton and Deputies Arne Sand and Ken Anderson patrolling lonely county roads, looking for cattle mutilators, unidentified flying objects or anything else that might help solve the puzzle.

Sleep soon became a scarce commodity as the three men answered continuous calls from troubled ranchers who were losing cattle or from frightened individuals who had seen strange flying objects, bright lights in the sky or hairy creatures eight feet tall.

Even with the deputies' diligence in patrolling many miles of back country roads in the sprawling county, the mutilations continued. Disappointingly, mutilations always happened in an area where the officers were not.

"We wonder at times," Captain Wolverton said, "if those mutilating have some way of knowing exactly where we are."

The growing number of people who have multi-frequency scanners has made it possible for almost anyone to monitor law enforcement radio calls. One time the deputies obtained two older cars and an old pickup truck, tuned them to run well and equipped the vehicles with telephones in an attempt to patrol undetected. They used the vehicles six months, but were still unable to come closer to solving the mysterious happenings.

After his initial three weeks of working on the problem and realizing its complexity, Captain Wolverton called a joint meeting of the Great Falls news media and requested their help. He asked the representatives of the local newspaper, the four radio stations and the two television stations if they would be willing to put out a story asking area residents to cooperate by reporting any information they might have.

The appeal gained support and produced at least one unusual lead. A man in a nearby community phoned to say that his son in Minnesota was, as a sideline or hobby, assisting another man on research that might possibly link cattle mutilations with unidentified flying objects.

Captain Wolverton called the son, who mentioned a convict in prison in the midwest, who seemed to know quite a bit about it. After corresponding with the prisoner, Captain Wolverton and Deputy Arne Sand, who is a polygraph examiner, traveled to the prison and talked with the inmate.

The interview lasted six hours, but it was not as fruitful as the lawmen had hoped. The prisoner failed some of the polygraph tests Deputy Sand administered and a later investigation of the information the convict supplied proved that the information was false.

Part of the story related by the convict was that a contract to kill several Montana government officials was in existence. He said explosives were to be used to blow up a city block in the capitol city of Helena. Later the prisoner changed the location of the predicted disaster to Havre.

Although Captain Wolverton did not believe the convict, he took the precaution of notifying the Governor's office on his return. The explosion, which was to have taken place before October 1, 1975, never occurred.

Throughout their long months of investigation the members of the Cascade County Sheriff's Department have had the total cooperation and assistance of a number of professional men, each an authority in his own field.

These professionals include several area veterinarians who went to the scene of mutilations, examined carcasses, did autopsies and gave their professional judgment as to possible cause of death, methods of mutilation and other pertinent information.

Despite their professional skill, they were unable, in most instances, to determine the cause of death. However, they were in total accord that a very sharp, possibly surgical, instrument was used to remove sex organs, the rectum, teats, lips and other parts of the animal. On more than one occasion they theorized that the incisions appeared to have been made by someone with an extensive knowledge of anatomy or medical training.

Invaluable assistance in the investigations was rendered by a Montana pathologist who made numerous tests at the request of the Sheriff's Department. An animal pathologist in Colorado also was consulted on one occasion to examine hide removed from a mutilated animal. These men verified some important new clues, but the significant question of who or what caused the mutilations was still unanswered.

A Montana toxicologist has made innumerable tests on specimens taken from the mutilated animals, as well as grass and other substances found in the area. When he determined further research beyond the capabilities of his laboratory equipment was desired, he called on the assistance of a number of other labs in other parts of the United States.

Laboratory tests were also made by the state university system and an area hospital.

Although the sheriff's departments in each of the five counties have investigated individually, they have also shared information. In some instances they have assisted one another in investigations, mutually attempting to solve the mysterious events.

Leading the investigation in Teton County is Sheriff Pete Howard. Undersheriff Jerry Skelton is handling mutilation investigations in Judith Basin County, Deputies Bob Blades and Tom Lee are working on cases in Chouteau County and Sheriff Walter Hammermeister is conducting the investigative work in Pondera County.

Other counties in Montana that have had isolated reports of mutilations are also sharing information with Cascade County.

Air Force officials have been cooperative, particularly since the rash of UFO and unidentified helicopter sightings began.

The public, as a whole, has been most cooperative since Captain Wolverton's public appeal through the media. There are some persons, however, who have been reticent to report anything strange or unusual, primarily because they fear their friends' ridicule.

The Sheriff's Department has continued to solicit reports from any residents who see or hear anything strange, because each incident may add another piece to the jigsaw puzzle officers are trying to complete.

Montana lawmen have also worked with officers in other states where mutilations and strange sightings have occurred. They have wondered about the significance of the fact that most reported mutilations have been in western states. This may be because of the large number of cattle in these states and the distances with low population density.

Of all states, Colorado appears to have more mutilations and Cascade County officers have conferred a number of times with Colorado lawmen.

Of particular interest to the Montana officers was a news release concerning a statement by Governor Richard D. Lamm of Colorado.

Dated August 25, 1975, the news story said in part: Governor Richard D. Lamm flew to Pueblo Monday afternoon to confer with the executive board of the Colorado Cattlemen's Association concerning the widespread livestock mutilations that have occurred throughout the state.

Calling the mutilations "one of the greatest outrages in the history of the western cattle industry," Lamm pledged the full resources of the state to help stop the mutilations and arrest the persons responsible.

"It is no longer possible to blame predators for the mutilations," Lamm said, "It is clear from the evidence that only human predators can be responsible for these terrible offenses."

The Governor noted that the School of Veterinary Medicine at Colorado State University had concluded that mutilations were being caused by humans using knives.

Reports from other states include mutilation of a pig in Minnesota and cattle in Texas and South Dakota. A sheriff in South Dakota wrote to the Cascade County Sheriff's Department asking for any information concerning offenses in your area as to the modus operandi.

Considerable information and copies of files were exchanged with law enforcement agencies in other states where mutilations have been reported.

Lawmen continue to ponder why almost all of the reported cattle mutilations in Montana have been in the five-county area around Great Falls, including Cascade, Chouteau, Teton, Judith Basin, and Pondera Counties.

Of course, they theorize, it is possible that other areas are having the same problems but they are unreported. And in many areas, reported mutilations are labeled as predator-caused.

When highly trained investigative officers work on a problem for almost a year and are unable to come up with a solution, there has to be a factor, yet undiscovered, which is necessary to solve the mystery.

4

MONTANA IS NOT ALONE

Were livestock mutilations in other states following the same pattern as those in Montana?

Had law officers in these states come up with any substantial evidence that might be helpful in solving the mutilations in Montana?

These were some of the questions Captain Wolverton considered when he started contacting law enforcement agencies in other states where mutilations had taken place.

The replies were interesting, but did not solve the riddle. Some reports indicated a similarity in incidents, while others introduced entirely new bits of information to add new and baffling parts to the puzzle.

The reports of two mutilations in Meeker County, Minnesota, were particularly interesting. One involved a cow and the other a pig.

The cow was mutilated with blood removal similar to those in Montana. The interesting aspect was that law officers arrived on the scene shortly after the cow was mutilated and although there was about a half inch of snow on the ground, the area in a six-foot radius immediately around the cow was melted off. Officers were unable to find any footprints or car tracks.

The pig mutilation also had a strange aspect. The farmer who owned the pig told authorities that his yard light had gone out and he had assumed that it had burned out. About 20 minutes later, the yard light went back on.

He went outside the next morning and found the mutilated pig in the barnyard. It was mutilated in a manner similar to most incidents involving cattle.

The officer who reported to Captain Wolverton said there had been 12 mutilations south of his county toward St. Paul. It was noted that birds and predators did not feed on mutilated animal carcasses.

Until the pig mutilation, all information the Cascade County Sheriff's Department accumulated involved cattle. However, shortly thereafter, in mid-August, a report was received that nine sheep had possibly been mutilated near Red Lodge, Montana. The left ear had been cut off seven of the sheep. Two of them died, but the remaining lived.

Interesting information concerning mutilations in Colorado was published by the Colorado press. While investigating a cattle mutilation, a Sheriff in that state found an Army bag containing a scalpel, surgical gloves, and a bovine penis at the scene. It is possible that these specimens were purposely left at the mutilation site.

The Sheriff at Sioux Falls, South Dakota, shared a number of reports on mutilations occurring in late 1974, after the first incidents reported in north-central Montana, but before the major rash of mutilations.

An incident in late September, 1974, regarding a Black Angus heifer was similar in several ways to the mutilations that later occurred in Montana. The heifer's tongue and reproductive organs were removed, and the excision was completed in an almost perfect circle, with no jagged edges. It looked as though a precision instrument of some description was used.

The right ear was removed in an unusual method. The report stated that the ear was not sliced off at the skull's surface, but the entire ear was excised from the skull.

As in most Montana cases, no blood was on the ground by the animal or on the skull and no tracks were found around the animal. A tuft of hair, presumably the animal's, was found about two feet from the rear of the animal. It was in ball shape and approximately tennis-ball size.

Lawmen there contacted the Sheriff of another county in Minnesota who reported two mutilations similar in appearance, except that these were mutilations of male animals instead of female.

Another mutilation near Sioux Falls involved a one- or two-day old calf that had all internal organs removed. All that remained of the calf were the backbone, hide, rib cage, head and legs. The tongue, the left ear, part of the nose, and the bull calf s testicles were removed. There was a hole about one-half inch in diameter wherein the hide of the left shoulder of the calf was removed.

Investigating officers found no evidence of the internal organs being dragged along the ground as would be the result if a predator had taken the organs.

Apparently the absence of tracks puzzled the South Dakota officers too, who reported that in one investigation the mutilated heifer was found in the middle of a soybean field which had been harvested. The ground was very soft, but no tracks were found.

A man in Texas who has apparently been assembling data to help law officers in their investigations of cattle mutilations sent Captain Wolverton photostatic copies of reports and news articles collected from a number of states. The man said he worked with the knowledge and approval of his local sheriff and asked that Captain Wolverton send him information about mutilations in Montana.

Among the information the Texas man submitted was a

copy of the poster advertising a $2,000 reward for information leading to the arrest and conviction of those doing the mutilations. The reward was offered by the Wisconsin Livestock Protective Association, organized in 1970, and which has over 250 members.

He also submitted copies of news stories telling of the mutilation of a cow in Kansas, the organization of a farmer-vigilante group in Nebraska and a $500 reward offered by the American Humane Association in Denver, Colorado.

A news broadcast over a Salt Lake City television station in the fall of 1975 stated that there had been 1,600 mutilations in 28 states. Whether this figure is accurate or not is not known but news-paper stories have reported cattle mutilations in a number of states including Texas, Oklahoma, Washington, Oregon, Minnesota, North and South Dakota, Kansas, Colorado, Nevada, Utah, Wyoming and Idaho, as well as Montana.

In addition to checking with law enforcement personnel in other states, Captain Wolverton contacted a man in Nebraska who is a doctor of pharmacology and a bio-chemist, to get further information on the effects of certain drugs on livestock.

The man verified that Ketaset is an anesthetic or tranquilizer. He said Ketaset was the name used when the drug was still in the experimental stage.

The man voiced the opinion that the two holes found in the jugular vein on many mutilated animals could have possibly been used to inject a salt solution through the one hole while pumping out the blood through the other. He added that the salt solution could not be detected after the animal was dead any length of time.

Meanwhile, reports of mutilations continued to come into

the Cascade County Sheriff's Office. One report stated a calf was found dead in a remote area of the High wood Mountains. The calf was missing both ears, its male organs, tail, rectum and tongue. Captain Wolverton cut its throat and found no blood in it or on the ground around it.

On the ground directly in front of the calf was a white substance forming an X measuring 10 by 17 inches and topped with a bar. Officers wondered if it could be some sort of a symbol, so they sent some of the substance to a Missoula laboratory for analysis. Disappointingly, the substance turned out to be bird droppings.

Judith Basin County Undersheriff Jerry Skelton investigated the mutilation of a bull calf in which a hole had been drilled in the back of its head and the brains removed.

In some cases, the cause of death was definitely not attributed to mutilation; for example, a cow and calf found near Simms. A veterinarian did autopsies on both animals and said the cow died of emphysema and the calf expired due to intestinal blockage.

The mutilation of a cow south of Stockett followed what seemed to be the usual pattern-rectal area, tail and one ear removed—but there was one difference. A white, filmy substance, similar to that discovered earlier on a mutilated calf near Utica, was found on the hair of the cow's neck. It was sent to a laboratory for analysis, along with samples of the soil around the animal at 2 feet, 9 feet, and 20 feet. Although extensive tests have been made at the lab, the white substance has not been identified. Scientists did confirm that it is not petroleum distillate, as in the other case.

A mutilation with a different twist was investigated by officers February 20, 1976. The cow, found northwest of Cascade, was dead an estimated one to two weeks.

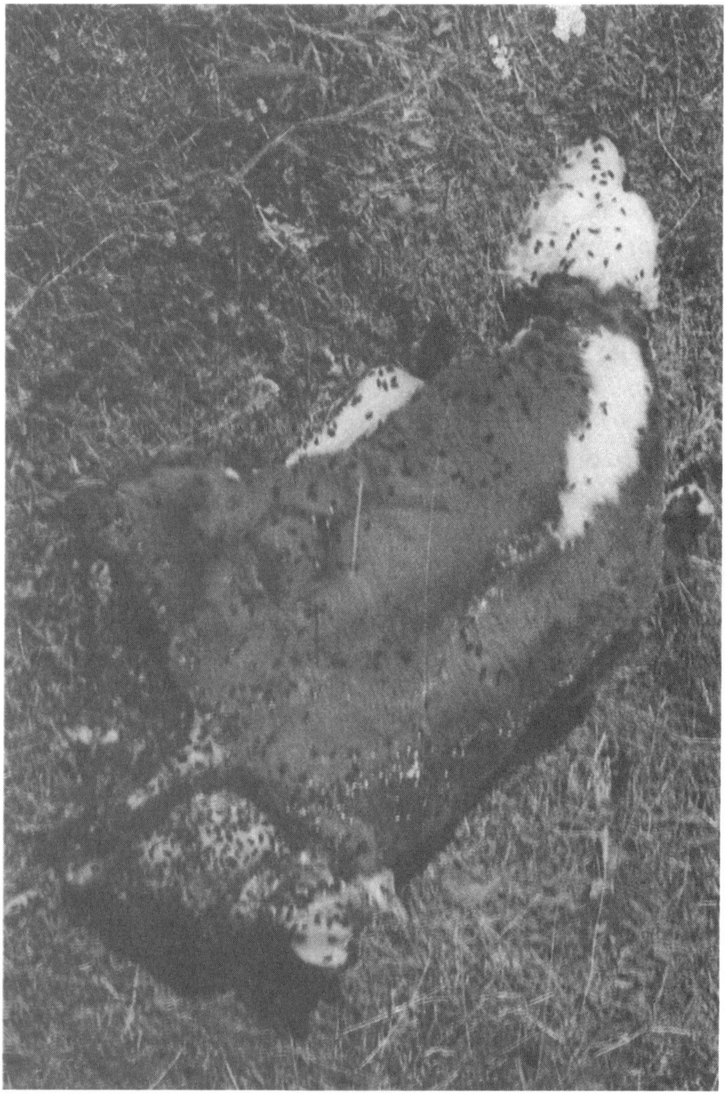

There was no blood in this mutilated calf when the investigating officer slit its throat. Nor was there any blood on the ground around it. However, it was missing both ears, its male organs, tail, rectal area, and tongue.

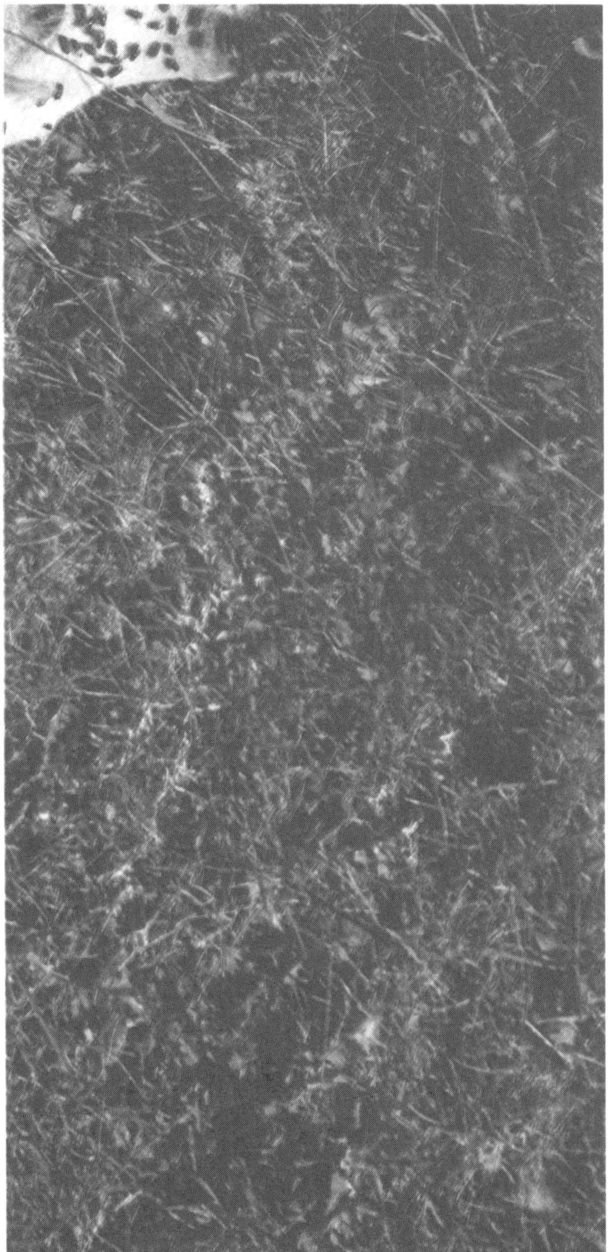

Directly in front of the mutilated calf (previous photo) officers found a large X formed by some white substance. Thinking it could be a symbol, they sent a sample of the white substance to a laboratory for analysis, but it turned out to be bird droppings.

Two circular patches of hide from the belly, one teat, and one ear were missing. Apparently the carcass had not appealed to birds of prey, as there were no droppings or other evidence that birds had eaten on it.

In examining the carcass, Captain Wolverton cut open the throat, revealing no blood, but he found an extremely foul-smelling, milky fluid which ran from the opening. Some of it was sent to a laboratory for testing, but the tests did not determine what the fluid was. However, a veterinarian later said it was possibly putrefaction of tissue.

As in most cases, there were no tracks around the dead cow.

One of the greatest dangers in any investigation of strange or frightening circumstances is the panic it can cause when people hear about it. Such was almost the case at a rural high school in Cascade County one day in October, 1975.

A rumor was going around the school that humans were to be mutilated next and that on that particular night some residents of the area were to be mutilated.

The Cascade County Sheriff's Office was notified. A special assembly was called at the school and Captain Wolverton and Deputy Arne Sand drove to the school to speak to the students. They explained that there was no validity to the rumor.

The deputies found out in questioning the students later that the rumor was started by some of students as a joke.

The officers did not consider it funny, as they knew what fear and panic can do to normally stable citizens.

5

THE MONTANA SITE

Ideas are sometimes rejected by human beings simply because those ideas lay beyond the realm of their acceptance.

Ideas that seem too far out are discounted as fantasy, labeled impossible or simply ignored.

The Cascade County deputies, working to solve the rash of cattle mutilations, felt no idea was too weird to merit careful consideration. For this reason, they have considered the theory that the mutilations were the result of some cult and they expended considerable time investigating reports that might indicate positive confirmation of this theory.

"Some people believe the theory that mutilation is done by devil worshipers," Captain Wolverton said, "and we don't discount it. It could be true."

There has certainly been evidence that could indicate this is the answer. And if a cult is responsible for the mutilations, it would explain in part why the blood is often drained from the animal and certain parts of the animal removed.

About two months after Captain Wolverton started investigating the mutilations, he discussed them with a law officer in another part of the state, who had moved to Montana about two years earlier.

The officer said he believed the mutilations involved a cult of witches. He told Captain Wolverton that he had information but was reluctant to talk about it.

The officer's theory was that the cattle were being tranquilized with PCP, a hallucinogenic drug. The blood was then removed from the animal and given to the witches of the cult to drink, which caused them to trip out.

The time sequence when the mutilations take place has a significance, according to the theory advanced by the officer. He said he believed the cattle were killed when the sun and moon were in a certain phase which could explain why so many are during a full moon, or that mutilations occur on a cult member's birthday or on certain days such as the spring equinox.

The officer's theory is shared by a police officer in another Montana city. However, at the time of this writing, it is not more than theory.

The cult theory was also advanced in a report the Cascade County officers received from a sheriff's office in California. The officer there reported that there had been mutilations in his area, but he did not know of any in which the blood was removed.

However, he reported that a group of backpackers saw members of a cult sacrifice an animal. He said the cultists were wearing hoods and robes and were chanting. When law officers arrived later at the scene, all that they found was the remains of an animal which had been buried.

There is a site in Montana, near Butte, which appears to be a location for ritualistic ceremonies. Law officers have learned that the place is referred to as the Montana site. Some authorities believe a cult occasionally holds ceremonies there during the full moon and the members of the cult are dressed in long robes.

Several law officers have visited the site, which is a short distance south of Butte on U.S. Forest Service land. The turnoff from the mountain road to the site is marked with a large stone with Nelo 5-15-29 painted on it in black. The site is about 75 yards up the mountain from the rock.

This is believed to be some kind of ceremonial site used by a cult or cults. It is located just south of Butte in the mountains. The area around the apparently natural pit is outlined with rocks of various sizes. Some of them have inscriptions on them which could be interpreted different ways.

A report by Captain Wolverton and Deputy Ken Anderson, who visited the site April 14, 1976, states: Approximately 75 yards up the mountain from the rock is a complete circle of rocks 61 feet in circumference (this is west of the Nelo rock). The rocks encircle what looks like a natural pit; it did not appear to have been dug out. The pit is 4½ feet deep with a fire pit at the center. The fire pit was encircled with small rocks about 18 inches in diameter. There was no indication of a recent fire, and when it was used the fire was very small.

Inside the encircled area are two Lodgepole pine trees, one on the right and one on the left. Each tree had a nail in it. If something was stretched between the two trees it would be off center and be over the stone with ISIS printed on it. The stone with the inscription of ISIS favor us! Mother of moon lover of goodness, is resting on the roots of one of the trees. If one were standing in the center of the pit looking at the ISIS stone, one would be looking southeast and the stone faces north-west. By drawing a straight line from the ISIS stone to the northwest, the line would be in the center of the rock that is inscribed with YHWH.

There does not appear to be any relationship between the stones that have writing on them and various rocks, selected at random, which have the painting on them. None of the rocks that made up the circle were very large—the biggest being roughly 10 inches across, the smallest being a handful of rocks to fill up any gaps.

Reports by officers who had visited the site earlier indicated there was a coyote trap near the stone labeled ISIS, but it was not there when Captain Wolverton and Deputy Anderson visited the site. ISIS is believed to be the name of an ancient cult of Egypt, later worshiped in Greek and Roman empires, which had as its symbol a cow. The cult was said to

This is the altar in the place near Butte commonly known as the Montana site. The stone, resting on the roots of the tree, is inscribed, ISIS favor us! Mother of moon lover of goodness. ISIS is Egyptian for mother of goodness but it also stands for an ancient cult in Rome, believed to have been involved in cattle mutilations.

have utilized mutilations in ancient times. ISIS was an Egyptian goddess of fertility.

The word YHWH on the rock opposite the one labeled ISIS is believed to be a forbidden pronunciation of the word God. The numbers 5-15-29 is numerology standing for evil and Satan.

A five-pointed star and a symbol similar to the Nazi swastika were found on some of the stones in circle. The star, called a pentagram, is a symbol of the Devil, and the swastika is a symbol of a cult.

Two stones bore the name Jesus. Another was labeled Ariel, which is one of the five satellites of the planet Uranus, which some believe has an evil influence. Another stone bore the inscription Jehova, which means female demon, but could also possibly be an abbreviation of the word Jehovah, meaning God. Several of the words had more than one translation and there are other interpretations that could be made of the site. One tube of black paint and a paint brush were found by one of the trees, but time and weather had eliminated any chance of getting fingerprints from them.

While Captain Wolverton and Deputy Anderson were there, a deputy from Butte and his trained dog searched the site and the immediate area around it, but found nothing.

An interesting incident took place on Forest Service land in Blain County, Idaho, and may or may not have a connection with cattle mutilations.

Two Forest Service men were placed on guard in a remote area to keep cattle from being illegally grazed on Forest Service land. Apparently one of the two men left to go into town and the other was standing guard from a secluded area where he could not be seen.

As he was watching, about 5:45 p.m., he noticed two men

dressed in body length black, hooded robes, walking about 50 yards from him. The taller of the two men was carrying a bag, but the guard could not determine if there was anything in it.

Although there was a jeep trail about five yards from where the men were walking, they apparently preferred to stay among some willows, as though to avoid detection. Their pointed hoods apparently had a partial opening, but they did not turn their heads so that the guard could see their faces.

When they reached a clearing they hurried, giving the impression they did not want to be seen. They looked straight ahead and never turned their heads.

One of the most unusual aspects of the incident was that cattle in the area became very quiet justbefore the strangely garbed men appeared. The guard said he was expecting an elk to appear, but instead these two men appeared. He told authorities that he observed the men for approximately three minutes.

Officers said no mutilated cattle were found at the time the two hooded men were seen, but they added that there had been numerous cattle mutilations reported in that county.

An interesting theory was advanced by a young woman who was interviewed by authorities in Montana. She claims to know that some very rich people are behind the mutilations and that they pay less wealthy persons to do the mutilation for them. She said they often pay from $500 to $1,000 for the parts taken from the animals.

Authorities have not proven or disproven her theory.

At one time during the investigation, Captain Wolverton corresponded with a man in Arkansas who has done extensive research in the field of ESP (extra-sensory perception). He had earlier helped the Cascade County Sheriff's Department in connection with a homicide case, but at this particular time was writing to Captain Wolverton concerning any possible connection between cattle mutilations, UFOs and the occult.

The man wrote that he had attended a conference on UFOs at which an investigator who was also a helicopter pilot stated that he believed the mutilations were the work of a fanatical religious cult equipped with helicopters and using special shoes which left no tracks.

Commenting on this theory, the ESP expert wrote, "While I have not put my mind on this mystery, I cannot conceive of anything one could put on the feet which would not show tracks of some kind. Without trying to be psychic for the moment, the fact that this mutilation of cattle has occurred in a number of other states suggests quite a well-organized group for cultists, if they are the cause. This (has) happened enough times to give farmers a chance to have caught them at it or to have sighted them."

He asked the question that if helicopters are being used, how are they able to get in and out without being observed? Montana law officers have received numerous reports of unidentified helicopters in the area, including some that are all black with no markings. There have also been reports of people hearing helicopters fly over their homes at low altitude during the night, but these people were unable to see them.

"It would be some operation," the ESP man wrote, "for a helicopter to hover a few feet above ground while some of the crew jumped out, did their mutilation of the cattle and then were hoisted aboard. That still does not explain no footprints or tire tracks being left behind. And what about dogs who may have been watching the cattle? What would they have been doing meanwhile?

"Indulging in fantastic speculation," he continued, "space

ships with their power to remain stationary in the air and occupants to float to earth, as has been reported, leaving no imprints, taking specimens of animal parts and blood for examination, etc., could come closer at explanation. It would seem it would take unusual instrumentation and devices for instantly making the cattle immobile, to do such a job and get away with it, in an incredibly short length of time. But who can accept such a speculation?"

The man asked if the farm area was being policed at night and if the farmers themselves were concerned enough to set up watches.

Captain Wolverton told him in his letter of reply that some ranchers had set up patrols, but nothing had come of it. Law officers also patrol the rural areas, but so far they have not been able to catch the mutilators.

The ESP researcher, who is himself a sensitive, described the ESP impressions he had received on the mutilations with these words:

"I feel, however it is being done, that there are bands of five—women as well as men involved. I see them masked, wearing black or dark jumperlike, tight-fitting clothing. Sinister appearing, highly trained in their operations, each assigned certain duties ... armed with guns and instruments ... equipped with black cases or specially prepared bags for carrying the animal parts ... containers for blood... they move in quickly, efficiently, and are away just as quickly. I get the feeling of air action ... what kind, I cannot "see" ... but it seems silent ... they have somehow "cased" the area and select time and place when they are almost certain of no detection."

The man admitted that the things he had heard or read about cattle mutilations could have colored the impressions he received.

But law officers wondered at the strange coincidence of the black outfits with the black-robed men in Idaho and the black helicopters seen over Montana.

6

LAW OFFICERS GO ON MERRY CHASE

The idea that helicopters were possibly being used by those mutilating was not new to the Cascade County Sheriff's Department. They considered this possibility many, many times.

But the thought had added emphasis when, in the late summer of 1975, they started receiving numerous calls from people who saw helicopters that could not be identified or heard strange noises, some like a helicopter, but saw nothing. There were also instances when they saw a helicopter, but could not hear it.

At almost the same time, the sheriff s office started receiving reports of UFO sightings and of strange bright lights.

Officers contemplated the possible connection between unidentified helicopters and cattle mutilations because on several occasions a helicopter was seen hovering over some cattle.

There was some question as to whether helicopter was an accurate description of the craft. In most actual sightings, the person seeing the vehicle described it as a helicopter, and a number of people saw them at close range. But some of the sightings took place on a day when the wind velocity was high enough that all of the Air Force helicopters were grounded because flying conditions were unsafe.

If Air Force choppers couldn't fly in such weather, what kind of a helicopter could? Some of the unidentified helicopter sightings have been by law enforcement officers themselves, or members of their families.

One of the first reports came from the wife of a former deputy. She told officers that she was in a bedroom in her home caring for her baby when she heard a noise approaching which she described as like some kind of machinery.

The noise became very loud, as though the object from which it was coming was located in her back yard. At the same time, she said there was a very bright light—or actually two beams of light-coming into the room where she and the baby were. She said the entire room was lit up. She described the top beam as red and the bottom beam as white.

After a few seconds, the noise diminished like a combine going down the field and the light left the room. The sound seemed to indicate that the object, whatever it was, had gone over the house. The woman ran to the opposite side of the house, but did not see the light or anything else.

Adding a strange quirk to the incident was the fact that the family dog that ordinarily barked at strangers failed to make a sound, despite the fact his kennel was located directly in front of the window through which the light had come.

The next day a man who lived in the same general vicinity phoned in to report that he had seen a set of red lights close to the ground. He said the lights flashed for about one minute and then he was unable to see them anymore.

He was baffled by the fact the lights were in an area where there was no road and they traveled in a southerly direction, which would have been impossible for a regular vehicle, since there was a ditch in the way.

Three days after the former deputy's wife reported the strange lights and sound, the wife of one of the present deputies called from her home near Belt to say that a helicopter had just flown over her house at tree top level. She said it circled their band of sheep, so she herded the sheep into the barn. She described the craft as navy blue with yellow lettering.

On checking with officers at Malmstrom Air Force Base, deputies found that the base had two navy blue choppers, but they had white lettering. After investigation, it was assumed that this helicopter, which was also seen by another resident of the area, had to be one of the Air Force choppers.

At this time the Cascade County Sheriff's Department started checking with the Air Force, other federal and state agencies, and private businesses to get descriptions of the helicopters that ordinarily flew over the north-central Montana area. A list was compiled to aid officers in trying to establish identification of the helicopters reported.

Deputy Arne Sand, who lives at Fort Shaw, west of Great Falls, was arriving home in the late evening of September 15,1975, when he heard what he thought was a helicopter directly overhead. Although it was a clear night, he was unable to see the craft. Judging from the sound, it was headed in a southerly direction, so he got back into his car and drove about a mile south and again got out of the car to listen. While he was standing there, he judged from the sound that the craft had flown directly over him.

The sound, Deputy Sand said, was not like any helicopter he had heard, but made more of a quiet whirr.

That same evening, a ranch couple living to the north of Fort Shaw, near Choteau, reported seeing a helicopter that turned off its lights and flew south as they watched. Whether it was the same one Deputy Sand saw a little later could not be confirmed.

About ten days later the Police Department at Lewistown, 100 miles southeast of Great Falls, notified the Cascade

County Sheriff's office that there were several helicopters flying over missile sites in that area with spotlights. A check was made immediately with Malmstrom and officials there reported that there were no Air Force choppers in the Lewistown area that night.

A few days later Undersheriff Jerry Skelton of Judith Basin County reported two cattle mutilations in his area, along with the fact that unidentified helicopters had been seen in the area the same date that the mutilations had taken place.

A heifer, killed southeast of Stanford, had two teats removed, a two-inch square of hide taken from the left side of the belly, all blood removed, and the female organs, bladder and tail were gone.

The second mutilation involved a cow on a ranch near Geyser, northwest of Stanford, toward Great Falls. This cow was missing the rectal area, lips, tongue, nipples and all but one of her teeth.

The second cow was apparently killed during daylight hours. It was verified that the cow was seen alive at 3:30 p.m. and the mutilation was discovered at 4 p.m.

A grey helicopter had been seen in the area between 3 and 3:30 p.m. A green chopper had also been seen circling the area between 4:30 and 5 p.m. There were also reports that two choppers had been seen running together that night. Undersheriff Skelton also received reports of yellow, green and silver choppers with no numbers on them.

It was later learned that a construction company working in the area had a large silver colored helicopter and a smaller yellow one with black letters. It could not be established whether these were some of the same choppers seen by individuals. Nor was it possible to definitely prove a connection between the helicopter sightings and the mutilations.

Farmers were growing uneasy and Cascade County deputies feared a situation might develop like the one reported in Colorado. That state had had many reports of sightings of unidentified helicopters, coupled with a rash of cattle mutilations and ranchers were threatening to shoot down any choppers they saw over their land.

Captain Wolverton went to the Air Force officials at Malmstrom and explained the potentially dangerous situation. He suggested that a spokesman for Malmstrom go on television and tell area residents just what the Air Force helicopters were doing, how they flew at low altitude to check lines between missile sites and the fact they were not in the air at night except for rescue missions.

Air Force officials were glad to do this and the result seemed to be a better attitude on the part of area residents.

However, reports of sightings, or sometimes "hearings," continued to come in, many of them with no logical explanation.

One man who was camping in Moose Creek Canyon near King's Hill southeast of Great Falls, told authorities a helicopter came through the canyon flying so low that it vibrated his mobile trailer, yet he was unable to see it.

A resident of the Milligan area, south of Great Falls, reportedly heard a helicopter in his area for an hour and a half, but couldn't see it.

Nine helicopters were reported flying together one night in the Hobson, Utica and Kolin area near Lewistown.

A man in Teton County reported that he, his wife, and their two sons watched a helicopter hover over their cattle one evening. The craft, with red and blue lights, was only a quarter of a mile away, but they could hear no noise.

A Sand Coulee woman told deputies she saw a black helicopter with no markings flying about 100 feet above her property. The bubble on the front of the craft was of dark or tinted glass, so she was unable to see inside. The sighting was during daylight hours.

A woman living near Great Falls reported that she was watching television when a helicopter flew over her home. She said it hovered and buzzed the area for about 15 to 20 minutes.

She recalled that the same thing had happened about a month earlier, but she had not reported the first incident. Checking revealed that there had been a cattle mutilation in the area at the time of the first incident.

The reports of helicopters hovering over cattle led Cascade County deputies to search further into any possible connection between the choppers and cattle mutilations. It was decided to do a little experiment, using an Air Force helicopter. A site was selected north of Great Falls, with the permission of the landowner.

Deputy Ken Anderson, the department's highly trained photographer, was lifted over the experimental area in a "cherry picker" device on a boom-equipped truck. He took pictures of the test area, which was marked with orange cones.

The chopper then came in and hovered over the area. As it flew off, Deputy Anderson returned to his "perch" to get an "after" shot of the area.

The first site was in grass ten inches tall. The procedure was then repeated over a dirt field, seeded to winter wheat. In both cases, the pictures taken after the chopper left showed no evidence of its being there. However, a shot taken after the chopper landed in the tall grass showed two eight by three-inch impressions left by the skids.

It seemed safe to assume that unless the helicopter landed, there was no way to prove it had been there.

An Air Force helicopter hovers over a field of tall grass. Photographs taken before and afterwards showed no evidence that the helicopter had been there. The experiment was performed to help check any association between unidentified helicopters seen in the area and cattle mutilations.

The same experiment was performed over a dirt field seeded to winter wheat. Photos taken by Deputy Ken Anderson showed no sign of the helicopter's presence earlier and it was assumed that a helicopter would leave no evidence unless it landed.

As reports continued to come in, Air Force officials at Malmstrom notified Cascade County officials that they would have two helicopters standing by with armed teams, ready to be launched if any helicopters were reported in the vicinity of missile sites. They agreed to keep the sheriff's office informed, if the crafts were launched.

This followed a report November 8, 1975, that several people saw a helicopter hovering over a missile site in the Lewistown area. A check was made, and no agencies had helicopters working there that night.

The night of Dec. 2-3 was a busy one for both Air Force and Cascade County officials as reports poured in of sightings of both unidentified helicopters and UFO's.

During the evening a report came in from the Juliet missile complex north of Malmstrom that a low flying aircraft, believed to be a helicopter, had been seen in the area. The airman who reported the incident, said the craft was so low at times that it appeared to almost touch the ground.

Checks with Malmstrom, Great Falls International Airport at Gore Hill and the Air National Guard, revealed no helicopters in that area.

Since the craft was headed north, toward Dutton and Brady, sheriff's offices in those counties were alerted. Eighteen minutes later the unidentified chopper was seen east of Dutton over the Diamond Valley Road. It was spotted again, 38 minutes later, over some Minuteman missile sites 15 miles north of Malmstrom. Thirteen minutes later, the aircraft was seen about ten miles out of Great Falls and headed toward the city.

In the meantime, about 45 minutes earlier, a law officer on patrol reported he was under the chopper and estimated that it was hovering at an altitude of 500 feet. He radioed in that the helicopter was taking off at a high speed, traveling toward Brady and that he was unable to keep up with it.

Air Force radar was unable to pick up the craft, but said that their coverage was only to the Dutton area.

Air Force officials then reported that there seemed to be more than one helicopter, as they were getting sighting reports from two different missile areas. All law enforcement cars were notified.

At 10 p.m., at the request of the sheriff's office, announcements went out over local radio and television stations asking anyone who had seen any helicopters, or observed them landing within the past half hour, to notify the sheriff's office.

The appeal brought an immediate response.

One man phoned in to say he had seen a helicopter flying over his ranch at tree-top level the night before. He said it had navigation lights, but no landing lights.

Another man, who declined to give his name, said he saw "something" land about a mile and a half north of Fairfield shortly after the time of the broadcast. It had one landing light, he said.

A Havre man phoned in to say he had seen a helicopter four of five miles northeast of Carter that had lights on and was moving toward Great Falls. A little after midnight, Malmstrom received a report that a helicopter was hovering about 300 feet above a missile site in the Conrad area. It reportedly moved toward Brady, then returned to the Conrad site.

An hour and 15 minutes later there was a report of a helicopter hovering over a missile site at Vaughn, directly over the overpass. A law officer sent to investigate said he saw a strobe light headed east, but was unable to verify if it was a helicopter. He talked with a sergeant at the missile site, who said the aircraft did not sound like a conventional helicopter and had only a single strobe light and no running lights.

Twelve minutes after the law officer saw the strobe light, it was reported by Malmstrom seven miles east of the base and headed in that direction. Seven minutes later, when it was within five miles of the air base, it disappeared. Radar units at both Malmstrom and Gore Hill tracked the vehicle until it disappeared.

A little over an hour later, Air Force officials again reported seeing what they termed a UFO with strobe light near Juliet, the same missile site 25 miles north of Malmstrom where one was seen the previous evening.

Eleven minutes later the sheriff's office received a call from a man who lived in the Highwood Mountains, east of Great Falls, saying he had seen a UFO there. This was in the same general area where the craft had disappeared a little earlier. Law officers were dispatched to investigate. The object was not visible on radar at Malmstrom.

In the meantime, the man who reported the sightings was contacted by telephone and he said clouds were starting to cover the object. He added that he had watched the object as it was close to the ground and it appeared to be more yellow than white. As it climbed, it seemed to turn white.

Despite the best efforts of both sheriff's and Air Force personnel, the frustrating game of hide-and-seek ended without any identification of the craft or crafts and no explanation of what they were doing except leading everyone on a merry chase.

7

CHASING LIGHTS IN THE SKY

Apparently whoever was at the controls of those unidentified helicopters the night of Dec. 2-3 enjoyed harassing law and Air Force officials, as the following night (Dec. 3) more sightings were reported. Officers were able to trace the crafts' course through a series of reports spanning a two hour and 40-minute period, but were unable to identify them.

This time the calls originated in Choteau and were based on phone calls received in the Teton County Sheriff's Office, as well as on reports of law officers and contacts with Malmstrom.

A Teton County law officer radioed in at 6:59 p.m. to report a helicopter south of Dutton and headed east toward Fort Benton. Five minutes later the officer said the craft was over the Juliet 11 missile site in that area.

A check with Malmstrom Air Force Base to determine if it was an Air Force chopper received a "negative" reply. The unidentified chopper, flying at low altitude, had a strobe light. Attempts by RAPCON (Radar Approach Control, a civilian agency) to pick it up on radar were unsuccessful.

At 7:40 p.m. the Teton County officer established that it was not one, but two, helicopters and at that time one was heading east and one west.

Eight minutes later another officer reported two helicopters over Bootlegger trail north of Great Falls, flying toward the city.

The helicopters seemed to multiply like rabbits. By 7:54 p.m. Malmstrom received reports of two helicopters over Juliet 5 missile site between Great Falls and Fort Benton (northeast of Great Falls) and two northeast of Conrad (which is northwest of Great Falls) traveling toward Fort Benton. This was basically the same general area as the sightings of the night before.

At 8:11 p.m. Choteau reported choppers south and east of Dutton, near the Teton-Chouteau county line.

At 8:33 there was a report of three helicopters with flashing red lights over the Juliet 5 missile site near Fort Benton. Within two minutes all had left the area and at 8:52 they were reported seven or eight miles southwest of the missile site.

Malmstrom's Wing Security verified that there were unidentified helicopters in the area.

At 9:40 that evening two helicopters were reported ten miles north of Great Falls. Neither Malmstrom nor the tower at Gore Hill could confirm the report, nor could they identify the craft.

Deputy Arne Sand wearily summed up the evening's activity in his report, saying, "the office sent me north of Great Falls chasing lights in the sky again, and they were similar to the ones the night before. Again, was not able to see any shape of the objects behind the lights"

He was referring to his experience of the night before when he participated in the chase that took law officers over a wide area. At that time, he was sent to back up the Dutton town marshal, when he (the marshal) saw bright lights in the sky. What happened is related in Deputy Sand's own words in his official report:

"Between Power and Button a bright white light, about 500 feet above the ground came from the west and crossed the highway behind me going east. I was not able to see any shape of the object. For the next two hours the lights would come and go. At about 3:30 a.m., 12/3/75, Dick Gasvoda and myself were just arriving at Fort Shaw when the office called and said that some type of aircraft was hovering over the missile site at Vaughn, so back we went and when we got by the feedlots, west of Vaughn, we saw a bright white light over the feedlots, and it was going west at a high rate of speed. The object crossed the highway in front of us and headed towards Great Falls. I talked to the sergeant at the missile site and he said the craft was over the site with a bright light, but could not see any shape and did not sound like a helicopter."

Where to draw the line between unidentified helicopters and unidentified flying objects (UFOs) is difficult to determine. In some cases, the craft has been seen plainly enough to determine definitely that it looks like a helicopter. At other times, the bright light emitted by the craft made it impossible to exactly determine the shape or outline of the craft.

The method of flight often resembled a helicopter, but there were many more incidents when the speed and method of climbing was such that it could not conceivably be a helicopter.

And sometimes the viewer's description of what he saw ruled out the possibility of a helicopter.

Helicopter or UFO—between August, 1975, and May, 1976, the Cascade County Sheriff's office received about 130 reports of sightings in the five-county area.

There did not seem to be a pattern to the area where the sightings were reported and they ranged over a wide area.

Frustrated officers found that in many instances, by the time they reached the place where the sighting had taken place, the object in question was gone. It is difficult to investigate something that is no longer there.

Reports came in from many areas. The sheriff's office at Fort Benton reported a helicopter 20 miles east of that community. Malmstrom said there were no Air Force choppers in that area.

A woman at Eden told of a helicopter flying low right over her ranch home.

A resident of Chestnut Valley watched a helicopter flying for about an hour over the area where he lived.

An unidentified helicopter reported flying over Cascade, turned out to be one belonging to the Montana Air National Guard.

On the night of Dec. 4, immediately after the rash of sightings, which kept law officers busy for two nights, an officer saw a helicopter lift off from what looked to be the Deaconess Hospital landing pad at the southeast edge of Great Falls. He checked with the hospital's emergency room the next morning and was told that no helicopters had landed there during the night.

Late on the afternoon of Dec. 8 the sheriff's office received a report that a missile team had spotted a helicopter about 1,000 feet above Fox 10 missile site, west of Choteau and Augusta, in the mountains. It was also seen from Fox 9 and was believed to be headed toward that site. About an hour later Malmstrom notified the sheriff's office that there were lights on the ground two miles south of the Fox 10 site. There are no roads into this particular area, and, in addition, the lights appeared too far apart to be the headlights of a car.

At about the same time a Vaughn resident reported seeing three small helicopters flying in the area of Bootlegger Trail. He said one was at an altitude of about 50 feet and the other two at about 150 feet. All were dark colored.

A check with the NORAD command center showed no evidence of the choppers on radar. NORAD confirmed that all Malmstrom helicopters were in.

A short time later a report was received that a woman living near Portage had noticed some men around her farm machinery, but when they saw her they jumped in their helicopters and left. She told officers she saw two helicopters in a wheat field about 50 yards from the house.

A report was also received from the sheriff at Fort Benton, who thought one helicopter was flying toward Great Falls while another was down in the Portage area.

The mystery was solved—at least this time—when an officer in the Canadian Air Force phoned the Cascade County Sheriff's Department later in the evening to tell officers he was flying the helicopter that went down near Portage, due to engine trouble. He said he landed as near a residence as possible and knocked on the door, but no one was home.

Another Canadian chopper pilot came to his rescue, helped him repair his craft and they both took off for Malmstrom. The distraught residents who reported seeing the helicopters were informed by the sheriff's office that there was nothing to be alarmed about.

A few days later, Malmstrom notified the Cascade County Sheriff's Department that crews at a missile site near Ulm, south of Great Falls, had reported seeing three helicopters flying at 150 feet altitude around the site. They said they frightened one away by shining a large light on it.

Sheriff's officers were on their way to the site when they received a radio message to "disregard" as the choppers had been identified as belonging to the Army National Guard.

The incident was almost forgotten when it happened to come up in conversation sometime later between Captain

Wolverton and an Army National Guard official. The latter denied the choppers had belonged to the National Guard.

In some instances, the sightings of unidentified helicopters had a logical explanation, but in most cases they didn't.

Chouteau County deputies reported seeing two helicopters flying about 300 to 400 feet above the ground. They were described as having a large red light and a white strobe light.

NORAD confirmed no Air Force choppers were out and said they could not locate the crafts on radar.

Reports of unidentified helicopters continued to come in from different areas. RAPCON reported a chopper sighting between Ulm and Cascade on Dec. 22. And a Great Falls man reported hearing a helicopter fly over him while he was camped in Prickly Pear Canyon Feb. 18.

These and all other reports were recorded as officers continued to piece together the parts of a baffling puzzle.

8

TEENAGE GIRLS CHASED BY UFO

During their entire investigation, Cascade County officers have sought to verify any possible connection between the cattle mutilations and the reports of UFOs, unidentified helicopters, strange lights and noises and the hairy creatures. In some instances, there has seemed to be a connection, but it has been frustratingly difficult to prove.

A case in point is a cow that was mutilated in late July, 1975, on Ashlot Bench north of Fort Shaw. As in many other cases, the cow's teats had been cut off, apparently with an extremely sharp instrument.

But in contrast to other cases where there was no sign of struggle, or tracks or other evidence around the animal, the grass this time was trampled down in a nine-foot radius around the carcass. Although a sample of the grass was tested at a laboratory, nothing conclusive was indicated.

But what particularly interested officers this time was the rancher's report that he was a red light blinking in a field where the cow was later found. He watched the light take off down a road. At the time, he said, he thought it was a highway patrol car. When officers checked, they verified that there were no highway patrol or sheriff's cars in that area at that time.

A short time later, a rancher's young son was out irrigating on his motorcycle when he saw a red light going through a field. It aroused his curiosity because he knew there was no

Cattle stand just beyond the trampled grass around a mutilated cow, but will go no closer. This incident, which happened near Fort Shaw, was unusual because the grass was trampled down. In most instances, there were no tracks or other evidence of whoever did the mutilation.

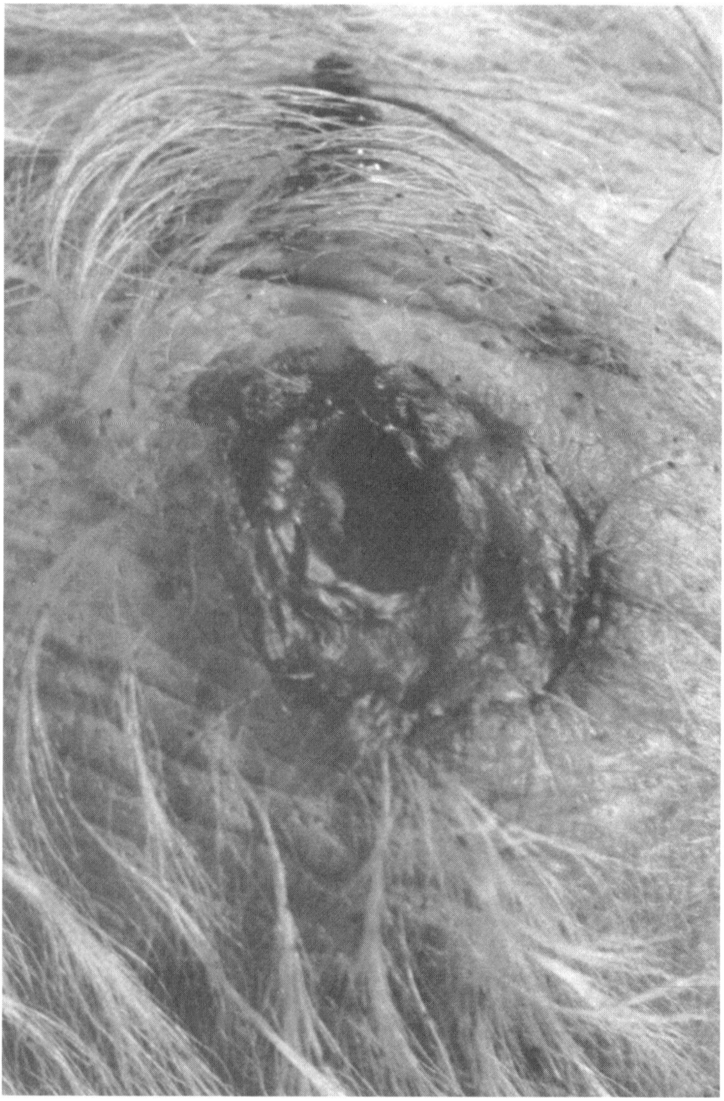

This photograph shows the area where the cow's teats were removed in a mutilation case near Fort Shaw (see precediing page). The hide area appears to be burned.

way for a vehicle to get into that field. Since his motorcycle was running, the youth was unable to say whether there was any sound coming from the object with the red light.

Shortly thereafter, the rancher discovered that two of his cows were missing.

They have never been found.

Later, one of their neighbors who had a cow mutilated also reported seeing a red light going down the road near the site.

The records in the Cascade County Sheriff's Office are filled with numerous reports of UFO sightings. In a number of cases, the person reporting the sighting was able to give officers a vivid description of the strange craft. These varied from a saucer-shaped craft or something that looked like a giant pear, to a large object that looked like a two-story building with lights resembling windows.

Often the viewer could see nothing but the bright light coming from the object. Officers explained this would be like meeting a car on the highway at night and being unable to describe the car because of the brightness of its headlights.

Sometimes a UFO seemed to chase cars or fly over airplanes. At times a strange object appeared to land, or to hover over a certain place.

A Raynesford farmer, reporting a UFO he saw, estimated the speed at which it ascended straight up at exceeding 5,400 miles per hour. When he first phoned in the report, Judith Basin County authorities suggested it could possibly be a bright star or planet in the sky.

"Then why can I see a mountain behind it?" he asked.

At least one person reported a daylight sighting of two UFOs and was even able to draw a sketch of what he saw for officers.

The man, who lives at Vaughn, a short distance northwest

of Great Falls, said he was driving on the interstate about dusk when he saw two UFOs flying from south to north.

He said each object had a domed top which glowed. There was a revolving blue and white light on the bottom of the crafts and lightning bolts as long as the craft itself came out of the bottom of one craft at intervals.

He said the two objects were not traveling fast and he was able to observe them for about five minutes.

Curiously, the reports of UFOs and the reports of unidentified helicopters started coming in about the same time, in the summer of 1975, although there had been some isolated calls before that time. It is obvious that the two are not the same thing, since eyewitnesses have described both the UFOs and the helicopters, and they bear little resemblance. Some of the bright lights, however, could conceivably be either one.

Two teenage girls, who live at Geyser, southeast of Great Falls, were badly frightened when they were apparently chased by a UFO as they drove home on the highway.

They told Judith Basin County UndersheriffJerry Skelton that they saw a strange object hovering over their car as they drove along the highway. It continued to stay above their car as they hurried home.

When the badly shaken girls reached their home, they ran inside and told other members of their family. All of them went outside and viewed the UFO, still hovering above the house. It left a short time later.

Like some of the unidentified helicopters, some of the UFOs seemed to make no noise. A Fort Shaw man, who watched a strange blue and white light among some trees near his home, told officers he heard no noise at all. A veterinarian, who incidentally helped investigate some of the cattle mutilations, was driving south of Bowman's Corner when he saw a

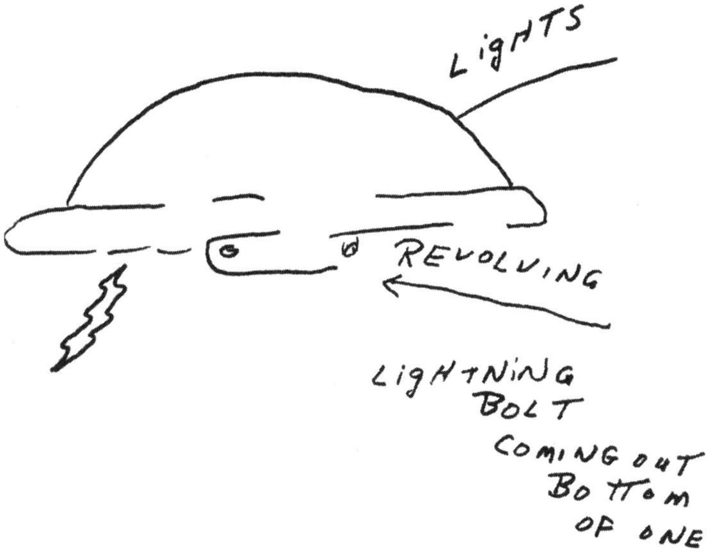

This sketch was made by a Vaughn man of one of the two unidentified flying objects he saw as he was traveling on the interstate. He said the strange objects had glowing domed tops and there were revolving blue and white lights on the bottom of the crafts. One UFO had lightning bolts coming out of the bottom of it at intervals. The man told law officers he observed the two crafts for about five minutes. It was about dusk at the time.

strange white light in the sky, with a red light on the left side. He told officers the light kept disappearing and then returning. He estimated his distance from the object at five miles.

An interesting and possible significant sidelight to the veterinarian's report was his comment that the cattle in the area started bawling "louder than I have ever heard."

Two days later a Great Falls man reported seeing a very bright light early in the morning, about 6:30 a.m. He said the light seemed to be just southeast of Malmstrom Air Force Base. It reminded him of an aircraft's landing light, except it did not seem to be moving.

He discounted the possibility of it being a star, since he could see stars behind it. He watched the light for about 11 city blocks as he drove home.

When his mother-in-law heard about what he had seen, she went outside and watched it, too. Later, several other people viewed it. "I don't know when the light left," the man said.

The sighting may have been only a prologue because a little more than 36 hours later, Air Force and law enforcement officials put in a night they will long remember.

The series of sightings began about 9 p.m. the evening of October 18, 1975, and continued until 7:45 the next morning.

Base Operations at Malmstrom confirmed that they had reports on nine different sightings in the Cascade and Eden areas just south of Great Falls. At the same time law enforcement officers were getting reports from north of Great Falls as far as Shelby.

The first report received by the Cascade County Sheriff's office was at 4:20 a.m. and came from the sheriff's office at Shelby. Officers there reported they had a UFO in sight and that it was moving from one location to another at an extremely high rate of speed. They estimated the altitude from 2,000 to 5,000 feet.

Malmstrom officials were immediately notified and they replied that they had been receiving reports since 9 p.m. the previous evening. Both Malmstrom and NORAD confirmed that the object was not a conventional aircraft and asked that they be given all possible information on it.

They had a description when a Shelby officer phoned in at 4:53 a.m. to say that the object was very close. He described it as a "white light, red flame aft, green light on top, red lights on both sides."

About 15 minutes later Shelby reported that the UFO was climbing and headed west.

At 6:04 a.m. an officer patrolling in the Power area, a short distance northwest of Great Falls, reported seeing the object over Conrad, between him and Shelby. He said it kept changing color from red to white and kept changing altitude slowly.

The situation was growing tense, and the sheriff's office sent an officer to Base Operations at Malmstrom to help as radio coordinator.

In the meantime, the patrolling officer had reached Dutton as he traveled north toward Conrad and Shelby. He reported the object was very low and then suddenly shot straight up until it was fairly high. Eleven minutes later, at 6:30 a.m. he radioed that the object appeared to be heading east from Conrad and was more brilliant in color.

The sheriff's office at Shelby said the strange object had also been seen by Montana Fish and Game officials. Its location was estimated southwest of Conrad.

Twelve minutes later the patrolling officer reported the object south and east of Chester, between that town and Fort

Benton. This location is 40 to 50 miles east of the area near Conrad where it was seen 12 minutes earlier.

The officer said the UFO was gaining altitude and appeared smaller. At 7:29 a.m. another officer reported the object was still in view in the east. His sighting was the last one reported during the hectic night.

Air Force officials said the UFO seen in the Cascade-Eden area seemed to have the same features as the one seen farther north, except at one time a flame came from the bottom of the object, emitting small lightning bolt-type objects. This coincided with the description given earlier by the Vaughn man.

Some Air Force personnel apparently got a good look at the object as they reported that at one time their Air Force vehicle, which was in Cascade at the time, was not more than a mile from the object.

A woman who lives east of Great Falls near the High wood Mountains also had a close-up view of an unidentified flying object. Her sighting was October 17, the evening before the many sightings that kept law officers so busy.

Captain Wolverton interviewed the woman, who told of seeing a huge craft, as large as a DC 10, fly over her house about 10:30 p.m. She couldn't estimate its altitude, but said it was about as high as helicopters usually fly.

She described the object as having lights all the way around it and said she could hear no noise from it. She watched it for about 30 seconds from a window of her mobile home.

The woman's neighbor said she did not see the craft herself, but her son did. She added that the same evening, between 7:30 and 8:30 p.m. she and four other people saw something between her house and her neighbor's mobile home. She described it as a large green light with a white light behind it.

She said it came over a hill and down the valley by a haystack and then disappeared.

The huge size of the UFO coincided with a number of other reports from people who described what they saw as being as large as a hotel.

9

EGG-SHAPED CRAFT WITH ARMS

As UFO sightings were publicized by the news media in Montana, there was bound to be a number of honest mistakes by individuals who mistook an extremely bright star for a UFO.

A report of six UFOs near Raynesford turned out to be Venus, Mars and a constellation of stars. What two Great Falls girls thought was a UFO was believed to be a beacon light. A sighting near Fairfield was believed to be another planet.

But not all sightings could be explained that easily. In fact, most reports defied explanation.

There was the case of the UFO that paced a B-52. It was reported to Sheriff Pete Howard at his office in Choteau. He said a Montana Fish and Game Department employee told of watching a UFO fly above a B-52 as the plane was flying over Freeze-out Lake where the man worked.

The man said he first saw the B-52 and then noticed another light flying directly over the plane. Using his rifle scope to get a better look, he noted that the strange object seemed to be pacing the B-52. In a short time, the UFO climbed out of sight.

The B-52 was flying in an easterly direction, he told officers.

The same evening the Cascade County Sheriff's Office had a firsthand account of a UFO sighting when Captain Wolverton and Deputy Anderson saw one as they were returning to Great Falls from Missoula.

If either of the two men had blinked his eyes, he might have missed seeing the strange object, as it was traveling so rapidly it was within their range of vision only four seconds. The dull orange or tan object passed within a quarter of a mile of the front of their car, at an elevation of about 500 feet. It was traveling from north to south-southeast.

The two officers said it was impossible for them to determine its size or shape in the brief time they saw it.

A couple of nights earlier Malmstrom notified the sheriff's office that two UFO's had been sighted south of Moore in the Lewistown area. The objects appeared as a bright white light with a whitish beam descending toward the ground.

About this same time the Cascade County Sheriff's Office learned that a woman at Stockett had observed a UFO hovering in the sky for a period of from one to two hours. She said it appeared to be a flashing red and white light.

Apparently UFOs come in different colors as reports have varied in this respect. Law officers at Chester reported seeing a UFO, that had green and blue lights, ten miles southwest of that community.

A Great Falls man, traveling on the freeway by Ulm, said he and his friends saw a UFO with a red light and a green light. The object appeared stationary.

A state official, while traveling one evening, reported seeing UFOs near Fort Benton and north of Carter. He said both of them cast a bluish light.

Perhaps one of the most unusual descriptions of a UFO was given to Teton County Sheriff Pete Howard by a ranch couple in that area.

They had an excellent opportunity to get a description of the craft as it was about five-eighths of a mile from their house and they watched it through field glasses. They also had the advantage of daylight, since it happened about 4:30 p.m.

They described the craft as egg shaped with the large end on the ground. It had one light which had a dull glow and then became brighter. They described the light as yellowish gold or light orange.

The most unusual part of the description was the fact the object had two appendages which came out of it, one on each side. The two arms made a continual motion, like a breaststroke. The craft remained stationary for five minutes, then the appendages retracted into the craft and it went straight up and out of sight.

The possible connection between UFOs and cattle mutilations again came to the forefront when a Simms rancher reported that his wife and children had seen a UFO land near the place where he had left a dead calf. He later discovered that the carcass had been mutilated after he placed it there.

There were actually two UFO landings at the ranch—one on December 8 and one the following night. The second incident was the same night that Captain Wolverton and Deputy Anderson sighted a UFO as they were traveling home and the same night that the B-52 was paced by a UFO.

The rancher was reluctant at first to talk about the incidents for fear people would think he was "silly." A little later, realizing the seriousness of the situation, he gave officers a full report and encouraged his wife to tell them about the extraordinary happening, too.

The calf died about five days earlier. The rancher had dragged it down into a brushy area near the Sun River, about a half mile from the house. The area was inaccessible by road except by going through the ranch-house yard.

On the evening of December 8, about 6 or 6:30 p.m.

the rancher's wife and children was a UFO land in the area where the calf s body was. They said it descended from the air, stayed down a short time and then took off in a westerly direction toward Augusta.

The woman described the object as a large white light with a red light on top. When it ascended, she said it appeared to roll on its side, as the red light was no longer on top, but on the side. As it left, it was flying at a low level.

The object, or one like it, returned at almost the exact hour the next evening. This time it stayed only about one minute, and instead of heading west, it flew east.

Captain Wolverton and two other deputies, after interviewing the woman, examined the dead calf. The bag area had been removed and the cut marks around the wound were consistent with those found in earlier cases that pathologists had verified were made with a very sharp instrument. Samples of the hide were sent to a laboratory for analysis.

The rancher verified that there were no marks on the calf when he had last observed it, two days before the first landing.

He told the officers that he planned to go home from work early, load all his weapons and wait for the "thing" to shoot it down.

Three deputies returned to the house the evening of Dec. 10 with photographic equipment so that they would be prepared to get pictures should the UFO make a third landing.

They were disappointed, as nothing happened.

About ten days later another report of a UFO landing came in from the Lewistown area. An Air Force missile crew, traveling between Roy and Fergus, northeast of Lewistown, late at night, said they saw an object on the ground that was glowing and pulsating. They reported watching it for five to ten minutes.

The Fergus County Sheriff's Office at Lewis-town was notified and a deputy went out to investigate, but he was unable to find anything.

A couple of nights earlier, the Air Force had some hectic moments when an unidentified flying object was sighted over Fairfield and was tracked on radar for about an hour and a half.

The oblong-shaped object was first locked in on radar at 8,000 feet. A little later it was fluctuating between 9,000 and 18,000 feet.

A commercial airlines plane flying in the vicinity was contacted by NORAD to see if visual contact could be made, but the pilot was unable to see it.

Within a short time, the radar contact was lost but law officers working in the area could still see the object. Radar contact was again made, locking the object in at 14,100 feet as it moved very slowly in a northwesterly direction. The object was also located by radar equipment at Havre. Air Force officials said the object was in the Power-Fairfield area, but they could not pinpoint it any better.

At one point during the tracking, when the UFO was in the Dutton area, radar showed the object suddenly ascending vertically from 14,750 feet to 44,400 feet at 850 knots or approximately 1,000 miles per hour and then stopping suddenly.

This maneuver startled military officials and law officers.

A few days later another Cascade County deputy had an opportunity to see a UFO, as Captain Wolverton and Deputy Anderson had.

Deputy Barry Michelotti and two friends were on a hunting trip and were camped in the Ford Creek area near Augusta.

Describing the incident, Deputy Mitchelotti said, "we were sleeping in my horse trailer that night with two horses tied to the back of the trailer. About midnight I was awakened by the horses. They were creating a disturbance, pulling back on the ropes, whinnying and pawing the ground. I looked up and noticed an object, described best as an object shaped like a football. This object was a solid white light, no flashing, glare or any beams of smoke or light. The object was at least five times as large as a star and was moving horizontally across the sky heading north. I woke up one of the other fellows and we watched it for a few short seconds. It was moving at a very rapid speed. After it left our sight, I checked the horses and one was missing. I heard it down the road running. I called and it returned but it was very nervous which is unusual for this horse. Both horses simmered down and there was no further trouble."

Captain Wolverton got a second look at a UFO on January 17, 1976, but again it was a brief one. He was driving at dusk on the lower river road just out of Great Falls when he saw an orange or amber colored light traveling from east to northwest. It was going so fast that he was only able to see it one or two seconds.

He checked with Malmstrom, but they had nothing on radar.

Just a week earlier, on January 10, a Belt area rancher noticed two red lights over his barn and corral as he was driving home along a country road. It was about 11 p.m. When he reached the approach to his place, he stopped in order to take a closer look at the lights. He noticed the red lights were pulsating and then a bright white light appeared, beamed toward the ground.

The rancher rolled down the window of his vehicle to try to hear whatever it was, but there was no noise coming from it.

The white light went off and the object started to move north. It went a distance, then stopped and the white light came on again. It disappeared, shortly, to the north.

The rancher described the craft as about 25 to 30 feet wide and said it appeared to be about 500 feet above the ground.

He checked his livestock, but they seemed all right and were not restless.

The incident made him recall something that had happened a couple of months earlier. During the night a bright white light lit up the interior of his home, waking his son and a friend who had been sleeping with him. The boys told the rancher, who went outside but was unable to see anything unusual.

On the same day, and in fact the same hour that Captain Wolverton saw his second UFO, a Great Falls man had an unusual experience at his ranch west of Augusta. The man reported that he was outside when he happened to notice, out of the corner of his eye, a strange object in the sky. He described it as pear shaped, about the size of a very large light bulb and a very bright incandescent type of color, almost like a ball of fire. He said it was traveling about 60 to 70 feet off the ground in a west to east direction.

The object appeared to burn out directly over his yard. "At the end, pieces seemed to fall off the tail of it and burn up and the whole thing appeared to burn up in the manner that I visualized a large ball from a Roman candle," the man told authorities.

He said his first reaction was that it was a meteor, but as he thought about it, he decided it would have been dropping to the ground, which this object didn't do. He commented that it was odd that the object, while in flight, seemed to maintain the same altitude at all times while he observed it, which was over a distance of approximately 100 yards.

A few seconds after the object burned up, the man heard a sonic boom a distance away.

10

ONE BIG ONE, FOUR LITTLE ONES

It was about 6 a.m., two days before Christmas, as a young woman was driving to work at the Great Falls International Airport. Although it was the season of the year for bright lights, she was in no way prepared for what she saw.

As she topped the hill where the airport is located, she saw a strange craft that was either on the ground or barely above it. The size of the egg-shaped object, she told authorities later, was "as large as a two-story building." It had three red lights in a cluster on top, she said, and there were windows in the bottom part.

Suddenly the strange object took off from in front of her car. It appeared to fly beside her for a time and then headed down the valley toward the city.

She had watched it for a total of about ten minutes, giving her a pretty good opportunity to see what it looked like.

When she related her strange experience to one of the men in the Federal Aviation Administration tower, he admitted that he had seen it too, but he wasn't going to talk about it!

The young woman felt differently. "I saw it and it was there and I don't care who believes me!" she told law officers.

Less than an hour later, at 6:45 a.m., another woman who works at the airport also saw something strange in the sky over the airport. Whether it was the same object as the previous woman had seen could not be established.

The second woman said the craft had two bright white

lights on each end and a triangular blinking red light in the middle. It seemed to be hovering a little higher than the airport tower and she estimated it was about three blocks away.

After watching the object for about five minutes, she went on in to work as it continued to hover over the area.

Perhaps seeing UFOs was beginning to be "old hat" for her, for it was her second sighting that month and both times were at the airport. On Dec. 11, as she was coming to work about 7 a.m., she saw a strange object, ahead of her and beside the overpass. She said it seemed to be about ten feet above the ground and was stationary.

As she slowed down on approaching it, the UFO took off rapidly toward the west and soon disappeared. She had observed it for about three minutes.

Drawing a sketch to illustrate what she saw, the woman told officers the large, oblong object had red lights on the sides and threw light beams to the ground. She added that it was definitely not a helicopter.

Reports of UFO sightings continued to come in and one of the most unusual incidents was that of a Fairfield area rancher, who described a "hotel size" UFO that was accompanied by four smaller ones.

The man told authorities that he and his family were returning to their home west of Fairfield about 9 p.m. the night of January 21,1976, when his two teenage sons noticed an object in a field near their home. Using two pair of seven-power field glasses, the family watched as four separate crafts, identifiable only as lights, seemed to cavort among a grove of trees about three-quarters of a mile away.

The rancher was interviewed by law officers and he related, "By this time these lights were coming back and forth out from behind this row of trees. And they appeared at that time to be landing in the field and so forth. So we watched them for quite a while, probably twenty minutes there with the field glasses on.

"About this time we saw two red blinkers down on the highway and I said, 'Well, somebody has reported it and the sheriff or somebody is out there now with a patrol car watching them, so we'll go on down, too.'

"So I took the two boys and jumped in the pickup and as we turned the corner off our approach onto the main highway, why these red things that we thought were patrol cars they then floated off the highway over into this field still blinking, or they were then. So we drove on down there and then as we approached the field where they had gone, why we saw this structure that looked like a hotel. Two-story hotel sitting out there in the field and the other lights were grouped around it. About four sets of lights grouped around it."

The rancher said the larger object appeared to be sitting on the ground. Although he could not make out the outline of the smaller objects, he said with the field glasses he was able to see the outline of the large UFO. He said it was a rectangular shape about 300 to 400 feet long and 60 feet in height, with two rows of windows, five to six feet high and two to three feet wide.

He added that he did not see anything moving inside the large UFO, but it gave the impression it had a very brilliantly lighted interior.

As he and his boys watched, the smaller objects came close to the large UFO, hovered about it, changed places and darted away, only to return again. He said they seemed to be affiliated with it, but he did not actually see any of them enter the large object or any come out of it.

Occasionally some of the smaller objects would land in the

stubble field. When they did, their light seemed to fade and grow dim and they actually seemed to shrink in size. As they watched, the objects would flare up and become very bright. The rancher compared them with an acetylene torch and said that it would hurt a person's eyes to look at them very long. At their largest size, the smaller UFOs appeared to be ten to 15 feet in diameter.

At one point the man and his sons saw what they thought was a helicopter with flashing red lights approaching. "We said, 'Well, here comes a helicopter to look at this stuff,' the man told officers. "So it came right over the field and no helicopter. And then my boy said, 'That ain't no helicopter, it's just another one of those, isn't it?' And I said, 'Yes, it is.' "

As they watched, the newest arrival tilted on its side while flying, revealing that it was flat on one side and round on the other, like a ball cut in half, or half a sphere.

Slowly and gradually, the "hotel" UFO started moving away from the viewers and disappeared over the horizon, into the Sun River Valley.

The smaller objects stayed in view for perhaps another 45 minutes as the man and his sons watched, and then they too disappeared in the same direction as the larger UFO.

The rancher and his boys got back in their pickup and drove farther down the highway, where they came upon a group of six small UFOs in a field. They believed this was a different group than the first ones they saw because the others had gone directly south and these when they left, went east and south.

At one point, one of the objects started up the highway toward the pickup truck. "My youngest boy said, 'Dad, that one's going to come right over us, right on the highway,'" the farmer related. "But it didn't. It veered off and went back out in the field again."

He estimated that it came as close as 100 to 200 yards before turning. During all the rest of the sighting, the closest the man and his sons were able to get to the objects was about 500 yards.

He was asked if the presence of the UFOs affected his motor, and he replied, “Never affected the lights. Never affected the motor or anything like that.”

At one point he shut off the lights to try to get a better view of the UFOs.

The incident was not the rancher’s first experience with UFOs. He told officers that about 14 years ago he saw one in approximately the same location. He said it was large and similar to the “hotel type” he had seen this time, but it did differ in that its windows were round instead of rectangular.

He said he did not tell anyone except his family about it that time, but this time, he said, “I don’t really care if anyone believes this or not. So I’m going to tell you what I saw.”

A report of a UFO landing came in from the Simms area February 5, 1976, and for the first time in their long and frustrating investigation, officers arrived on the scene in time to see the object for themselves. But they were thwarted in their attempts to get a closer look.

The call came in from a woman who was caring for some neighbor children while their parents were on a trip. She said she and her own two daughters were returning home from Simms when they saw a bright light behind the house and up on top of the hill. The woman stopped the car and they watched the light, which was very intense and pulsated when it was moving. It appeared to change color from a dull glow to a bright reddish orange.

She described the object as about 300 feet long with rows

of continuous lights along the top and bottom. She said the bottom lights pulsated alternately from left to right.

One of the girls she was caring for, a 16-year-old, saw the glow from a second floor window of her home.

After moving back and forth, the object left in a southwesterly direction, disappearing behind some buttes.

Shortly after officers arrived on the scene, they received a radio message from Sheriff Pete Howard, saying the lights were visible in the Sunny Slope area near Fairfield, not far from where the rancher and his two sons had watched the UFOs.

They were able to see the light, but, because of the hilly terrain, could not get closer to it. After two hours of trying to get closer, they lost sight of it entirely.

Teton County Sheriff Pete Howard received a report approximately two weeks later from a family who lives in the Rocky Mountains west of Choteau.

While telling Sheriff Howard about a UFO they had seen the morning of Feb. 22, the couple also said they had seen UFOs on at least five other occasions and some of their employees had also seen some.

Most of the appearances were around 7 o'clock in the morning. In the case of the Feb. 22 sighting, the man had just stepped out on the upper deck of their home to put up the flag when he noticed a very large object moving very slowly. It had apparently come out from behind one mountain and was starting to go behind another mountain peak.

In his excitement the man said he called to his wife and children to step outside and see it, but there was some delay as they didn't know at first what he wanted and then they had trouble getting the door open. He estimated he watched the object for about 30 to 40 seconds, but the rest of the family, only ten seconds.

The man said he didn't have an opportunity to get field glasses, but he described the object as large and elliptical in shape. He said it seemed to have a row of lights around the circumference.

The incident was the fifth time since the first of the year that the couple had seen UFOs. In one instance, the object appeared to be very low, in a canyon. Three sightings were in the mountains and the others on the flats below.

The couple pointed out that each time they had seen a UFO was on an extremely windy day with very little cloud cover.

It was one of many reports.

A Havre woman told how she and her son, while traveling near Chief Joseph Battleground, saw "an enormous ball in the sky." She described it as bright kelly green with a tail of gold sparks like fireworks.

A Helena woman wrote about seeing a gigantic light that lit up the entire western sky when she was driving near Helena.

On the same Sunday evening of early March, 1975, two Belt women, returning home separately from Great Falls, each saw an unidentified flying object near the highway.

The one woman, who was traveling alone, said she saw a white light, as big as her car, hovering over her about 20 feet above the highway. She told officers she drove the rest of the way to Belt at a high rate of speed, hoping to attract a highway patrolman.

The other woman had her two teenage daughters with her. At first, she said, they thought the bright light they saw was a helicopter, but when they got closer to it and it remained stationary, they decided it couldn't be a helicopter.

The egg-shaped object had two lights beamed from the front of it to the ground, but the three people watching it were mystified by the fact there was no circle of light on the ground where the beams were shining.

The woman told Captain Wolverton that at first she was extremely frightened, but suddenly a strange feeling of calm came over her and the two girls. One of the girls even laid down in the seat of the car in order to look up under the object, which was close beside the highway.

As suddenly as it had come, the feeling of calm left them and the woman said she "floorboarded" the car and got home as rapidly as possible.

To corroborate their story, she had each of her daughters and herself separately tell her waiting husband what they had seen. Each told the same story, although the girls had a few more minor details. "I had to drive, you know," the woman said.

Both women waited until some time later to report the sightings, but the incidents took on added significance when the dates were checked and it was learned that a calf was mutilated apparently one or two nights before.

The place where the first woman saw the UFO was in the immediate area of the mutilation, while the second sighting was about four miles away.

Another unusual experience was related to law officers by a Bozeman man. He said he was driving south of Augusta just before dark on February 6, 1976, when he noticed a car about a half mile behind him. He said the area was flat with no turnoffs from the highway. He had been looking into his rear-view mirror frequently, and this car seemed to "appear out of nowhere."

He said the car followed him for six or seven miles, so when he came to a turnoff, he pulled off to wait for it to go by. There was a dip in the highway just before the turnoff and he waited for the car to come out of the dip, but it didn't.

He finally continued on down the road and the car appeared again. When he reached Bowman's Corner, he pulled off again and waited for it to go by, but again it never appeared.

By strange coincidence, the same thing happened to his employer on an earlier night, in almost the exact same spot.

11

HAIRY CREATURES, EIGHT FEET TALL

Law officers have been unable so far to find an explanation for the sequence in which the strange events have occurred.

First there was the rash of cattle mutilations, then the many sightings of unidentified helicopters, followed by numerous UFO sightings and—more recently—the reports of people who saw one or more strange hairy creatures that walked upright like a man.

There was overlapping, but one type of activity seemed to decline as another started. Was it a piece of the puzzle or purely coincidence? Speculation seemed futile.

The first report officers received of the hairy creatures came Dec. 26, 1975, from two very badly frightened junior high age girls. One girl, who lives in Great Falls, was spending the Christmas holidays with another girl in the Vaughn area, and it was here the incident occurred.

The girls told the deputies that in the late afternoon they noticed the horses were acting very strangely, pawing the ground and rearing on their hind legs. They went outside to see what was the matter and it was then they saw a strange creature, about 200 yards from their mobile home and 25 yards or so away from a thicket.

The Great Falls girl found a .22 rifle belonging to her friend's father and looked through the scope at the creature. She described its face as "dark and awful looking and not like a human's." The girls said the creature was seven to seven and a half feet tall and twice as wide as a man.

To see if she could frighten the creature, the girl with the rifle fired it into the air. When nothing happened, she waited a short time, and fired into the air again. The second time the creature dropped to the ground and pulled itself along with its arms for a short distance before standing erect once more.

The girls decided they had seen enough!

They took off running, intent on finding someone who would take them to Great Falls, where they could wait for the Vaughn girl's mother to get off work.

One of the girls looked back over her shoulder and saw several other creatures—she thought three or four—helping the first one back into the thicket.

The girls swore their story was true and their obvious fright reinforced what they had said. Later they both willingly took a polygraph test which further indicated they were telling the truth.

The night following the incident, Undersheriff Glenn Osborne, Captain Keith Wolverton and Deputy Dick Gasvoda went to the area to search for the creatures or any evidence. While Undersheriff Osborne and Deputy Gasvoda went into the brush to try to "flush them out," Captain Wolverton waited in the clearing with a starlight scope, which permitted him to see in the dark.

No creatures were found, but the men did notice a number of trees broken off in the area, which is a similar observation noted at other sites where the creatures were seen.

When officers questioned the Vaughn girl's father later, he told of a hair-raising experience he had had shortly after midnight Christmas morning. He said he had awakened to a sound that he could only describe as like a human dying an agonizing death.

He said he took his flashlight and rifle and went outside to check, but his dog refused to go with him.

The awesome sounds have been reported in connection with seeing strange hairy creatures in several places in the United States. The Cascade County Sheriff's Office has tapes of the sounds from California, Pennsylvania and Washington.

It's an eerie sound, to say the least, officers have noted.

Reports from some areas where the biped creatures have been seen say that they emit an unpleasant odor compared to rotten eggs.

Not satisfied with their night search of the area, Captain Wolverton returned the next day and walked the area where the creatures were seen, but he found no footprints. The following day he flew over the area and took pictures of it.

In a telephone conversation with a writer in another state who was writing a book on the strange creatures, Captain Wolverton was told that reports of sightings have come from all over the United States. The writer said he had been told that the creatures do not leave tracks, that they have been shot at but it apparently doesn't hurt them, plus at times the creatures appear transparent. He added the bipeds have been observed in connection with UFOs.

The theory that bullets don't stop them was evidently shared by a Great Falls man who gave officers a belated report of seeing a large, hairy creature while hunting coyotes on Bootlegger Trail in December, 1974. He described the creature as seven or eight feet tall and said it looked like a grizzly bear. He said he fired at it three times with his 30.30 and when it kept coming toward him, he left hurriedly in his car.

It was about one month after the girls' terrifying experience that a man living two or three miles west of Vaughn, reported hearing the same disturbing sound the Vaughn girl's father heard on Christmas Eve. He, too, likened it to the scream of a man dying an agonizing death. He said it lasted about five minutes.

He looked out the bathroom window, but was unable to see anything. His dogs, which are ordinarily very aggressive and bark loudly when anyone approaches, were standing next to the house, making faint barking sounds.

Early in February, 1976, a woman in Babb phoned to tell officers that she and her husband had heard the same kind of weird sound twice during the preceding summer. She likened the sound to a werewolf. Again, the dogs appeared to be terrified.

She said other residents of Babb had heard the sound, too, and she understood a man from Browning had seen "Bigfoot" on Logan Pass in Glacier Park the preceding summer. Authorities did not have the man's name so they could not check the story.

Captain Wolverton received a report from an airman on February 11, 1976, who said he had seen footprints in the snow that appeared to be those of an animal walking upright. The tracks, found in the vicinity of Beaver Creek, in the Rocky Mountains west of Augusta, had three toes.

The airman also reported that some of the green pine trees in the area were broken down. Deep snow prevented Captain Wolverton from reaching the area, but he did fly over it. However, he was unable to see anything unusual.

A few days later a Great Falls woman reported she had heard the strange sounds twice—once between Christmas and New Year's and once in January.

By far the most startling report so far and the one that produced the most evidence, was one from a 16-year-old Helena boy. When Captain Wolverton learned of the incident, he and Deputy Ken Anderson went to Helena to interview the boy and his family.

The youth told the officers that he had awakened about

4:30 a.m. the morning of April 4, 1976, and stood looking out his bedroom window for a time. The second story window provides a good view of the pasture to the east of the house.

At about 5 a.m., the boy told the officers, he saw a tall, hairy creature walking in the pasture, coming from the south, or right. He said the creature was taking long strides and his arms moved back and forth as a person's would.

The creature did not appear to have a neck but it was capable of turning its head and it appeared to be looking around. Except for its face, it was covered entirely with brown or black hair about an inch to an inch and a half long.

The youth was unable to describe the face, but said the forehead protruded out then upward to a rounded head. The nose looked pushed in. He didn't notice any ears. In some respects the description matched that given of strange creatures seen in Pennsylvania earlier.

When the creature moved, the boy said it walked very smoothly without stooping and did not appear to bend its knees much.

When the creature's arms were at its side, the arms were as thick through from front to back as its body. The creature's back seemed to go straight down to below the buttocks, without any curve at the small of the back. The youth estimated the creature's height at eight feet. He claimed he was misquoted in a newspaper account as saying the creature was ten feet tall, and he was upset over being misquoted.

As the boy watched, the creature kept walking until it was directly east of the house, at which time it was joined by a second hairy creature. The second one was about a head shorter than the first, but just as wide and the color was the same.

At this point, the boy related, the larger creature reached

down and picked up something dark colored, "about the size of a bale of hay." Something was flapping from the ends of the object which looked similar to a piece of dark plastic.

The larger creature handed the object to the smaller creature, who carried it.

The larger hairy creature then started walking straight toward the house. When it was within about 100 feet of the house, it looked directly toward the window where the boy was watching.

The boy vaulted downstairs to wake his father and the two returned to the window in not more than two minutes, but when they looked out the strange creatures were gone. Even the use of 10 power binoculars failed to reveal anything.

The boy appeared badly shaken by the ordeal.

Later in the day, the boy's sister found a track in the pasture. She and the boy covered it with wood until the next day when they made a plaster cast of it.

Captain Wolverton and Deputy Anderson made their own cast from the one the youth had. The track measures 17½ inches long and 7 inches wide and appears to have three toes.

The boy drew three sketches of the creature for officers. The drawings are on file in the Cascade County Sheriff's Office.

In talking with the boy's father, the deputies learned of another incident that happened 12 days before the boy saw the creatures.

The father said he was taking a bath when he heard something outside his bathroom window, dressed and went outside where he found a large print in the five inches of snow below the window. He said he couldn't make any shape out of it but on either side of the track and a little forward were two different scratch marks in the snow. Each mark had five scratches indicated in the snow.

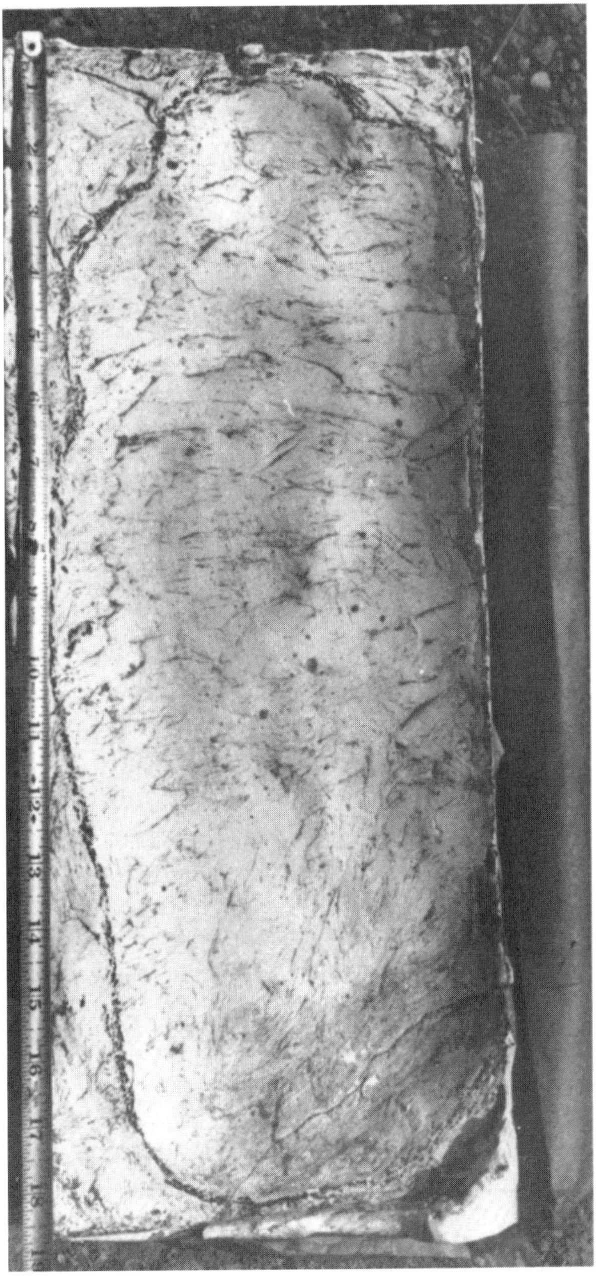

This is a photograph of a plaster cast made by a Helena, Montana, youth of a track found near his home. The track is believed to have been made by one of two large, hairy creatures seen by the boy in the pasture outside his bedroom window. Note the ruler that shows the length of the footprint as 18 inches.

A Helena teenager drew these sketches to show what the two hairy creatures he saw from his bedroom window looked like. He told law officers that one of the creatures came as close as 100 feet to his home.

The boy's mother also confirmed his story and added that during the two months previous a number of strange things had been happening. She told of hearing sounds like something heavy running outside and their dog being scared. She added that they had heard weird sounds like an elk bugling or dogs howling, both before and after her son saw the strange creatures.

The officers were also told that a 13-year-old boy who lives in the same area had also reported seeing one of the hairy creatures.

As officers searched the pasture area where the two creatures were seen, they noticed both cattle tracks and horse prints. When they asked the boy's father when the horses were taken out of the pasture, he replied, "There's never been horses in that pasture."

The boy said he had taken a lot of kidding about seeing the creatures, but he wasn't kidded by the officers. They did not doubt him, and Captain Wolverton added to his official report, "after talking to (the boy) and his family, I believe that (the boy) did see what he reported."

12

FALSE STORY FOOLS PUBLIC

Throughout the entire investigation, Cascade County deputies have meticulously sought to obtain the most accurate and factual information available. This has not always been easy, as memory plays tricks on people who are frightened or excited. And people find it difficult, sometimes, to describe something few others have ever seen.

Despite these obvious problems, officers have done everything possible to substantiate reports. They visited the scene of mutilations and sightings and searched for every shred of evidence. In some cases, they have questioned others living in the area. They also administered lie detector tests.

At times the officers personally knew the witness and could vouch for his reliability. And occasionally it was that sixth sense experienced lawmen seem to develop that helps them know when someone is telling the truth. It isn't always easy to spot a phony, but if anyone can weed them out, it often is a law officer.

However, there is at least one classic example of a man who told such a convincing (but untrue) story that he fooled not only officers but other people, including a writer whose story, based on the man's information, was published in a national magazine.

The writer, who wrote the story under a pen name, later told Captain Wolverton that he did not know at the time the information was false and he now regrets writing the story.

The information for the story originated with a man (referred to in chapter three) who was a long term inmate in a midwest federal penitentiary. It is not certain where he obtained his so-called "information," but the best guess is through the prison grapevine. His story had just enough accurate information in it, including names of individuals, to give it credibility.

According to the convict's story, the cattle mutilations were the work of a cult headed by a man in Texas. The man he named does exist but extensive checking failed to link him to anything out of the ordinary.

Cattle mutilations were only the beginning, the convict said. He claimed that the mutilation of humans was next, and had already started. He said that four people had been mutilated at Lake Kozad, Nebraska. Captain Wolverton contacted the sheriff there, who told him that no bodies had been found and there were no reports of missing people in that area. It was the sheriff's opinion that the entire story was false.

Cultists were doing the cattle mutilations, the convict said, to see if they could get away with it. If not detected, they planned to start on humans next, including a number of prominent people in the political field, news media and Hollywood actors. He had what he claimed was a list of 35 people who were to be killed, including some from Montana.

Captain Wolverton and Deputy Arne Sand, a polygraph examiner, made a trip to the prison to interview the convict.

Deputy Sand administered a polygraph test to the man, and he failed almost every question, including very simple ones. Checks made later on different aspects of his story all proved his tale false and none of the predictions the convict made have come true.

It was the officers, opinion after talking with the prisoner and checking his story that the whole thing was part of the convict's plan to obtain a release from prison or a transfer to a prison with less security.

In the meantime, the story caused considerable harm, as it had been reported by a number of newspapers as factual, including at least one newspaper in the north-central Montana area. Officers were concerned that the story would cause undue apprehension and even panic.

One curious aspect of the situation in Montana and other states is that the federal government does not seem to be doing any investigating of cattle mutilations. Or if it is, it is not sharing its information with local officials.

At one time during the investigation, Captain Wolverton received a phone call from a Department of Agriculture official in Washington, DC, inquiring about cattle mutilations in Montana. He indicated in his conversation that he was very interested and said he would fly to Great Falls the following week to confer with the Cascade County Sheriff's Department on the incidents.

Captain Wolverton and Deputy Anderson worked frantically to assemble copies of all of their reports and photographs for the man.

He never arrived, nor was there any further communication from him.

The absence of any federal investigation into something so important to the safety and welfare of the American public has made law officers wonder whether or not someone in high circles knows what is behind the mutilations, UFOs, and other mysteries, but is not disclosing this information.

"Call it a gut feeling," Captain Wolverton said, "but I have a notion somebody knows what is going on."

The theory is only a wild guess, but it could explain why official Washington seems to be ignoring the entire situation.

If the federal government is ignoring the situation, some private organizations of national scope certainly are not. One in Pennsylvania has investigated several hundred incidents in that state and a spokesman for the group told Captain Wolverton over the telephone that "there is no doubt the things are for real."

He added that UFO sightings have been reported in many places in the world and have increased in recent months. He also ventured a guess that there was a link between the cattle mutilations and the strange hairy creatures that have been seen in several states.

The reports of hairy creatures received in that area, the spokesman said, have come from responsible people, some of whom were not well educated and live in back country where they would not have read newspaper accounts of similar incidents.

One man reported shooting one of the "creatures" from six feet with a double-barreled shotgun. He reported that it "disappeared in a flash of light."

In some instances the strange creatures have been seen carrying small animals in their arms and some have been seen in the same vicinity and at the same time as UFOs.

The creatures have been seen in populated, as well as wooded areas, although they seem to prefer the latter. Some have been described as having "glowing eyes" and people have reported that the creatures had a pungent odor resembling rotten eggs. Some have been seen swimming in water.

As in Montana cases, the man said otherwise aggressive dogs seem immobilized with fear and fail to bark at the creatures.

One theory being studied by those at the Pennsylvania center is that the creatures may be a psychic phenomenon, visible to some and not to others and possibly non-physical.

This could at least explain why some people describe the creatures as transparent, report that bullets do not stop them and tell of the creatures disappearing before their eyes.

Another organization which is doing extensive research into the strange creatures, operates out of New Jersey. A man formerly affiliated with it in that state is now a deputy sheriff in southwestern Montana and is coordinating Montana's investigation with that in New Jersey. He told Captain Wolverton that in one recent month a total of 244 substantiated reports of UFOs were received in one county in Pennsylvania. That area has been plagued for three years, he said, by numerous reports of UFO sightings, followed by cattle mutilations and then sightings of the hairy creatures.

Comparing reports from various parts of the country, it is discovered that the "creatures" vary in appearance, but all have some similarities. They are reported to have anywhere from three to five toes, in some areas they have canine-type fangs, and the estimate of their size has varied.

A man with a research society in Michigan, in a telephone conversation with Captain Wolverton, said he once shot a "creature," which screamed and then disappeared into a swamp. He said the track it left was five-toed and measured 15 inches long and ten inches wide. The impression in the ground was one and a half inches deep.

The New Jersey organization is now using computers to study the information assembled thus far on UFOs, hairy creatures and mutilations. One conclusion reached, is that the incidents seem to happen mainly on hot, humid days in that area.

In any case, the incidents are taken seriously by those investigating them and every effort is being made to solve the mystery.

However, in all the checking Captain Wolverton and the Cascade County deputies have accomplished here and elsewhere, there have been absolutely no reports of any human being having been harmed by the "creatures."

13

UFO REPORTED IN 1897

Many people look upon the sighting of UFOs as something that has happened only in recent years. But there was at least one such incident almost 80 years ago, according to a story in a newspaper published at that time.

The strange episode reportedly took place in mid-April of 1897 on a farm in Kansas and involved the theft of a cow by the UFO, right before the farmer's eyes!

The news story, published in the Woodson County Advocate of April 23, 1897, relates the following incident, as told by the farmer, Alexander Hamilton of Vernon:

"Last Monday night about half past ten o'clock we were awakened by a noise among the cattle. I arose, thinking perhaps my bulldog was performing some of his pranks, but upon getting to the door saw to my amazement, an airship slowly descending over my cow lot about 50 rods from the house. Calling Gib Heslop, my tenant, and my son, Wall, we seized some axes and ran to the corral. Meanwhile the ship had been gently descending until it was no more than SO feet above the ground and we came up within 50 yards of it.

"It consisted of a great cigar-shaped portion, possibly 300 feet long, with a carriage underneath. The carriage was made of panels of glass or other transparent substance, alternating with a narrow strip of some other material. It was brilliantly lighted within and everything was clearly visible. There were three lights, one like an immense searchlight and two smaller—one read (red) and the other green. The largest was susceptible of being turned in any direction. It was occupied by six of the strangest beings I ever saw. There were two men, a woman and three children. They were jabbering together but we could not understand a syllable they said.

"Every part of the vessel that was not transparent was a dark reddish color. We stood mute in wonder and fright when some noise attracted our attention, and they turned their light directly upon us. Immediately upon catching sight of us they turned on some unknown power and a great turbine wheel about thirty feet in diameter, which was slowly revolving below the craft, began to buzz, sounding precisely like the cylinder of a separator and the vessel rose as lightly as a bird. When about 300 feet above us it seemed to pause and hover directly over a three-year-old heifer which was bawling and jumping apparently fast in the fence. Going to her we found a cable about a half inch in thickness, made of some red material fastened in a slip knot around her neck, one end passing up to the vessel and tangled in the wire. We tried to get her off but could not, so we cut the (fence) wire loose and stood in amazement to see the cow, ship and all rise slowly and sail off, disappearing in the northwest. We went home but I was frightened and could not sleep, but rose early Tuesday morning, mounted my horse and started out hoping to find some trace of my cow. This I failed to do but coming back to LeRoy in the evening found that Lank Thomas, who lives in Coffey County, about three or four miles west of LeRoy had found the hind legs and head in his field that day. He, thinking someone had butchered a stolen beast and thrown the hide away, had brought it to town for identification, but was greatly mystified in not being able to find any track of any kind on the soft ground.

"I went home that night but every time 1 would drop off

to sleep I would see that cursed thing with its big lights and hideous people. I don't know whether they were devils or angels or what, but we all saw them and my whole family saw the ship and I don't want any more to do with them."

The farmer's description of the craft bears a strong resemblance to those given by many who have seen UFOs in recent years. But what makes the 1897 account even more startling is that it happened almost seven years before the Wright Brothers made history with the first recorded airplane flight. And space travel was yet an undreamed of event of the future!

If the past was puzzling, so was the present, as reports continued to come in during the spring of 1976. Several incidents happened within a day or two of the first of May, which may or may not be significant.

Two cases of cattle mutilation were reported to the Cascade County Sheriff's Office April 29. One involved a cow belonging to a Castner Falls rancher. The Black Angus cow had been dead too many days for a successful autopsy, but it was obvious to the investigating officers that the tongue, an eye, an ear and the lips were gone.

The rectal area may have also been cut. The cow's head and neck had apparently been bent back at an angle to the right and a white fiber-looking substance covered one side of the cow. It resembled the petroleum distillate found on the calf in Judith Basin County, but laboratory tests proved it was not the same substance.

The other mutilated animal was a yearling steer belonging to a Simms area rancher. The rectal area appeared to be cut and there was what appeared to be a puncture mark on the right side of the carcass.

The veterinarian who performed an autopsy on the steer

noted that the steer had been eating up to the time of its death and had apparently been in good health.

An unusual factor, not encountered before, was a ruptured area, about four inches across, on the inside of the chest cavity. There was also a rupture the full length of the body on the animal's right side. The veterinarian commented that the ruptures were unusual. There were no external bruises.

Adding another note of mystery to the investigation was a report by a neighbor woman of the man who owned the steer that she had heard a "funny noise" three nights earlier, which frightened her. She said she was home alone, watching television, about 11:30 p.m. when she noted that there seemed to be a lot of traffic going by. She turned off the lights, leaving on the television, so she could watch for lights.

It was at this time that she heard an odd noise, which she described as a whirring sound, going on and off intermittently. It was not loud, but continued for about ten minutes.

Since the veterinarian estimated the steer had been dead two or three days, it is possible the noise the woman heard was the same night the steer was killed.

The night after officers investigated the mutilated steer (April 30) they received a phone call from a woman in the Fife area reporting a group of flying objects maneuvering over her community. She watched the objects through binoculars and said they appeared to have yellow, green and blue lights around the outside of the crafts and that their centers seemed to glow. They appeared to be headed south at a high rate of speed, she said.

She added that she had seen such crafts before, but had not reported them.

In a later conversation with the woman, Captain Wolverton learned that she often watches airplanes and helicopters and is familiar with them. She said she never phoned in a report unless she was unable to identify the craft.

A Great Falls couple, parked on a country road near Great Falls about 3 a.m. were badly frightened when they saw a UFO that did a disappearing act.

The incident happened about May 1, 1976, but was not reported until two weeks later.

The couple told Captain Wolverton that they had just parked on an approach road and turned off their lights when they noticed a small triangular-shaped object hovering about four feet above the ground very close to their car and ahead of it. It glowed with a blue light. They described the size of the object as about one foot by two feet.

When the car headlights were turned on, the object disappeared; when the lights were turned off, it appeared. The procedure was repeated three or four times but when the object seemed to be coming closer to them, the couple turned on their lights and engine and "took off."

The incident was similar to one Captain Wolverton had heard about in another state.

The strange sounds attributed to the hairy creatures cropped up again in a report to the Cascade County Sheriff's Office May 7. A man whose ranch is in the vicinity of Gore Hill, location of the Great Falls International Airport, phoned to say that he was out feeding stock early that morning when he heard a wailing-moaning sound. It was very loud and he thought it was close but could not determine the direction from which it came.

He said his horses acted strange and restless.

When Captain Wolverton played a tape recorded in the Puyallup, Washington area of the strange sounds heard there, the man said, "That is exactly what I heard."

Captain Wolverton and Undersheriff Osborne checked the area carefully but nothing was found.

The reports continued to come in and with them the theories and speculations. Some people have said in all sincerity that they consider the strange events signs of the second coming of Jesus or the end of the world, as foretold in the book of Revelation.

This theory, like the others, has been neither discounted nor endorsed by those conducting the investigation.

A man who is and has been a professional government trapper for 18 years was asked his opinion as to whether predators could have caused the mutilations.

He said that when coyotes feed on a dead animal they do not take the hide, nor will they start in an area where they have to break the hide. He said they would eat three to four pounds of meat in one or two days, but would not eat the entrails if any meat was exposed. He based his opinion on his experience in examining over 2,000 animals killed by predators over the years.

Investigating officers appreciate the comments of anyone who thinks he or she may have information which could possibly help solve the mystery. They are especially grateful to those cooperative residents who have reported cattle mutilations or sightings of UFOs or hairy creatures. Without this help, they would be unable to assemble the evidence that they hope will lead to an eventual solution.

"I want people to know," Captain Wolverton said, "that our department, under a directive from Sheriff John Krsul, is looking at this whole situation as serious."

Captain Wolverton urged anyone who might have something unusual to report to phone their local law enforcement officers or get in touch with him.

It is only by continuing to follow every lead, to investigate every incident, that lawmen will be able to solve the mystery of cattle mutilations and other strange incidents that are plaguing Montana and other areas.

EPILOGUE

This book, in a sense, has no ending. It can't have, as long as the story it tells is not complete.

At this writing, no one has produced proof as to who, or what is mutilating cattle, or why....

And although there have been many conjectures, some of them most convincing, no one has yet proved the identity and origin of the unidentified flying objects. Or the hairy creatures.

The mystery goes on and on, with new bits of the puzzle added now and then to further perplex those who are striving so hard to solve it.

One fact is certain. The officers in the Cascade County Sheriff's Department, from Sheriff John Krsul on down, take the strange incidents seriously and they are conducting a serious investigation.

They realize, of course, that there are times when a person's imagination plays tricks on him. And they also leave room to discount calls from pranksters.

But the men who have investigated the strange episodes related here have seen and heard too much to casually disregard it. They believe those persons who say they have seen hairy creatures or UFOs. In fact, some of the officers have seen UFOs themselves.

As for the cattle mutilations, the officers have observed too many strangely butchered cows to mark it all up to natural causes or predators.

There has to be an explanation for the strange and frightening incidents, and a solution to the syndrome of puzzling events. Those in the Cascade County Sheriff's Department have no intention of giving up before they unravel the mystery—no matter how long it takes.

They feel strongly that local sheriff's officers will probably be the people responsible for solving the mutilation mystery, when and if it is solved.

At that time, this book may have a sequel.

* * *

Editor's note: End of the original publication.

EPILOGUE

To the Updated Edition

Forty-three years ago Roberta Donovan and I put together the book, *Mystery Stalks the Prairie,* which tells about the mysterious events occurring around western Montana during the mid-1970s. At the end of our book, we stated our belief that these mysteries would be solved by law enforcement and, in particular, by the Cascade County Sheriff's Department where I worked.

It has not worked out that way. In fact, these mysterious events have now been investigated and analyzed nation-wide and internationally by universities, think tanks, and independent researchers such as Dr. Richard O'Conner and by Joan Bird, author of *Montana UFOs and Extraterrestrials.*

Dr. O'Conner and Joan Bird recently came to my home in Great Falls and interviewed* me and former sheriff Pete Howard from Teton County, who had worked closely with our office and had reports of similar events: animal mutilations (mostly cattle) and UFO sightings. It was their feeling that it was important to get our stories of events as they happened and as reported to us as sheriffs, for us to tell the tales while we are still here. Many who shared similar cases and experiences are no longer with us. My co-author, Roberta Donovan, has passed away, for example.

Therefore, I am writing this epilogue relating some of the additional investigations I've done since the publication of *Mystery Stalks the Prairie.*

**The transcript of this interview begins on page 171.*

In the early part of the 1990s, I retired. I had been a deputy sheriff since 1962 and during those early years I was involved in many types of investigations and police work like all sheriff's departments--disturbances, drugs, homicides, search and rescue, hauling prisoners around--just normal sheriff's duties.

Then things started to change in 1974. One of our deputies came to work and stated that one of his cows was lying down in his pasture. He found that the cow was dead and cut up. He looked for an explanation and found none. That's all he had to say. Soon after that, we started to get more calls regarding mutilated cattle. Most of these cases were written about in our book.

Having had a disagreement with the [news]paper who insisted that the mutilations were due to predators, and not being able to answer their questions and not answering my own, I believed I needed more information to understand the cattle mutilations, if at all possible. From the knowledge I'd gleaned, it appeared that these incidents were of an alien presence, and further investigation by many researchers has not proven me wrong.

After retiring, I knew I was never going to solve the cattle mutilations, so I decided to investigate the possibility of finding Bigfoot. There were Bigfoot sightings in Cascade County. A fellow researcher, Jon Andrews, and I started to look into all leads that came our way.

The first good story came to us by way of an elderly gentleman about a Bigfoot that he and several others had witnessed in California, in the famous Bluff Creek region. He had good credentials. He worked at the Jet Propulsion Labs and was very enthusiastic and down-to-earth relating his story while talking to us on the phone.

Jon and I made arrangements to meet and drove to California for the meeting. I think there were six of us, and we ended up near Bluff Creek. We all had tents. There were two from JPL, one a woman, also a man who was retired from Special Forces, and last a man who was from that area and was considered an expert guide.

The woman told me she had seen Bigfoot at the exact site about a week ago. She stated that a large fire was going at night and the Bigfoot came toward the fire. Everyone saw him. No one was frightened. The Bigfoot remained visible a short time, then left.

Our schedule seemed simple. We would sleep in and stay up most of the night near the campfire. Nothing happened except the talking about what had occurred in time past.

One day Jon and I took a drive around the area and met a camper who was having [vehicle] trouble. We were able to help him, and after introductions I realized that we knew each other through a mutual friend in British Columbia. He told us about two different sightings of Bigfoot in British Columbia. However, he had come to the Bluff Creek area because he believed that was the place to study them.

Jon and I returned to our camp and that evening we decided not to sit around. So we took a walk up a logging road. We stopped about a half a mile from camp and decided to stay there. It was very quiet and dark. Jon sat under a tree and I continued up the road.

After awhile I got bored with the silence and walked back to Jon. He said nothing occurred except he said he could hear what appeared to be a rock hitting the tree and falling down beside him. (It is not unusual to hear stories about Bigfoot throwing rocks).

We slowly went back to camp, still listening for any unusual sounds. After being back a short time, we heard a noise and someone said, "There it is." I listened to what I knew to be a truck going down a steep grade using his jake brakes. The sound came from several miles away. That ended the night. Nothing else occurred.

The next morning Jon and I awoke to hear some kind of argument. "You seem to think there's a Bigfoot behind every tree," said the Special Forces man to our guide. The yelling continued. The two of us packed up, said goodbye, and drove back to Montana, disappointed that only a thrown rock was any indication of Bigfoot.

Other Bigfoot trips took us to Washington state on several occasions, and to Oregon, British Columbia, Montana, and Alaska. In Eastern Washington we set up camp in the Umatilla National Forest. We talked with several people and heard a variety of stories, some claiming to have seen him; some saying he doesn't exist.

We did find some footprints that were very clear so either someone was playing a joke on us or they were real. We made several casts of these prints.

One man, Wes, was a packer and had many pack trips to the Umatilla area. His pack string contained horses and mules. One day he heard a rifle shot. The shot didn't concern him, but his pack string became upset.

Then, in Wes's line of vision, there was a Bigfoot coming down a hill with what appeared to be a wound in his shoulder. Wes could see blood coming out. The Bigfoot went to a creek and with his good arm dipped into the mud and put it on his wound. Leaving the creek, it went up a mountain pass and out of sight.

The next day Wes rode up to that pass and said he saw the Bigfoot lying in a meadow below him. For the next three days

Wes rode up to that pass. On the second day, the Bigfoot was still in the meadow. On the third day, it was gone.

Wes wished he could have seen more of the Bigfoot during its trip up the mountain after the shot. However, he was pretty busy keeping his pack string together. I know how fast a pack string could go to hell because I'd been in that position.

When Wes returned home, his wife handed him a local newspaper. There was a story about a man shooting a Bigfoot in the area that Wes had been in.

I know this is a strange story, but it was always told the same way. Every time Wes packed into those mountains he used the same color of stock and was always dressed the same, figuring the creature or creatures would recognize him and consider him okay.

Alaska was a destination we were interested in as one man, who marked trees for logging, found a large woven nest among a group of trees. Jon made arrangements with the Tlinget Native tribes and we were on our way. We ended up on Prince of Wales Island and stayed at one of the tribe members' homes and saw many tribal members come to the house. We felt we were being checked out, and we must have passed inspection.

After a couple of days, we were at the location where the nest was found, having been guided there by a young man who had been assigned by the tribe to be our guide. The entire area was closed before our arrival because of the nest.

The nest appeared to be five feet by four feet. It was interesting because it seemed to be woven into an oval shape by grass and twigs. Jon and I set up camp within sight of the nest, hoping we would catch sight of a Bigfoot, to no avail.

The man who found the nest had taken some hair samples from the nest. He turned them over to us, and Jon sent them to a lab. The hair turned out to be hair from a bear. Jon also located a book at the university library in Seattle that explained how certain bears do build nests. At the end of the Alaskan trip, I stopped looking for Bigfoots for the time being. However, Jon is still looking and if anyone finds the creature, it should be Jon.

Along with our investigation of the cattle mutilations [in the 1970s], I was also involved with UFO sightings. I am unable to explain the connection between the two mysteries, which occurred at the same time.

I and Under Sheriff Glenn Osborne would respond to the calls that came in regarding UFOs, and there were many. Some were just unusual lights in the sky. We never spotted a UFO, but we did however observe various unusual lights in the sky. Maelstrom Air Force Base was also eager to assist because many of the sightings were around missile sites. These sightings lasted for several months.

We were not the only state with unexplained mysteries. I live in Las Vegas sometimes and Great Falls other times. While living in Las Vegas, I received a call from Colm Kelleher, PhD., who represented NIDS, the National Institute for Discovery Science. It is a research program which is dedicated to studying unexplained mysteries. The first time I walked into the institute, I was amazed to find a huge map of Montana on the wall with pins denoting all of the reports of unexplained happenings, all of which had come from my book.

Colm had studied many unusual phenomena from all over the country. I eventually met with Colm and George Knapp, a renowned investigative reporter with television. It was determined that I could accompany them to a ranch in Utah called the Skin Walker Ranch. I'd heard unbelievable stories regarding the ranch. It had many mysterious events including cattle mutilations, Bigfoot, UFOs, and disappearing cattle.

Some of the things happening sounded like actions of poltergeists. The ranch was located under Skin Walker Ridge which is taboo to local native Americans. They would not go there nor would they go to the ranch. I spent two hours walking on the ridge and observed nothing but rocks and grass.

I would recommend Colm Kelleher and George Knapp's book entitled Hunt for the Skin Walker to get more information. This book is truthful and unbelievable. The reader either might become more involved in strange phenomena or might get rid of the book. You have to remember that everything was investigated by scientists, engineers, and former law enforcement officers. I don't know of any investigations that have attracted so many researchers.

Prior to my retirement, UFOs became part of my life. It seemed as though I was called out every day or night. I would pick up Under Sheriff Glenn Osborne, and we would go to the area with the hope of finding something unusual.

One such night we were patrolling the north part of Cascade County and radioed Sheriff Pete Howard [of neighboring Teton County], who was out looking for the same thing as we were. Glenn and I approached a missile silo. I turned on my red lights to identify ourselves, and we were met at the fence by a military man who explained that some strange lights were observed hovering around the missile silo. They were now gone.

We radioed Sheriff Howard who went to a mobile radar site and was invited to enter. The military personnel inside were looking at radar which indicated a UFO to the south of them. Sheriff Howard was able to look at the radar and saw the UFO. Then he was abruptly asked to leave by two men dressed in black. They told the sheriff that he would be receiving a call from the Air Force [in Colorado] the next morning. (That call never came, as was the case with other calls promised by government officials.)

Sheriff Howard then called us to see if we were still in the area. We explained that we were still at the missile silo. Pete said that there should be a UFO directly above us as noted by his observation at the radar site. We got out of the car, looked around and saw nothing. Typical. These occurrences happened so often that if the reported UFO was more than lights in the sky I would hurry to the sighting. I wanted to see a UFO, not lights.

So what was going on? The Skin Walker Ranch had many more situations and many more varied reports than Montana. Yet that ranch, with all of its investigators, scientists, and researchers, couldn't solve its strange phenomena, and neither could Montana solve its mysteries.

I am aware of UFO conferences in various states which are always attended by hundreds of people looking for the latest sightings and theories. There are libraries full of books on the subject and interest continues to grow.

No longer is it considered weird or crazy to believe in the existence of UFOs, and to think, as I do, that they are of an alien nature.

I am glad I was able to play a part in the early reporting of these events.

Keith Wolverton
January 31, 2019

INTERVIEW

"Are UFOs Real? Listen to These Montana Sheriffs!"

The 2016 YouTube Interview
with Keith Wolverton and Pete Howard

Keith Wolverton (left) and Pete Howard (right).

Editor's note: The following interview expands on the cattle mutilations described in Mystery Stalks the Prairie *and reveals several UFO incidents that occurred during the same period, including UFOs flying alongside Air Force bombers and hovering above nuclear missile sites.*

The video interview took place on August 3, 2016, with Keith Wolverton, retired sheriff's captain for Cascade County, Montana, and author of *Mystery Stalks the Prairie,* and Pete Howard, retired sheriff of Teton County, Montana. In the 1970s both men investigated cattle mutilations and UFO reports as law enforcement officers in adjacent Montana counties.

The interview was conducted by Dr. Richard O'Connor with assistance by Dr. Joan Bird.

Dr. O'Connor is a retired anesthesiologist in Helena, Montana, and is active in UFO research. He started the Jesse A. Marcel Library for UFO research and discussions in Helena. The library was named after the Army major who investigated the 1947 Roswell, New Mexico, UFO crash. For many years Dr. O'Connor worked with Marcel's son, also a Helena doctor, and often heard the son tell of his father showing him strange pieces of debris from the UFO crash site.

Dr. Bird, also of Helena, is a longtime advocate of the existence of UFOs and related phenomena and is the author of *Montana UFOs and Extraterrestrials* (Riverbend Publishing, 2012).

The YouTube video is entitled, "Are UFOs Real? Listen to These Montana Sheriffs!" and may be seen at youtube.com/watch?v=nR_hKWv45OY. The interview took place in Wolverton's home.

The transcript of that interview follows. It has been lightly edited for length and clarity.

* * *

Dr. Richard O'Connor:

I'm Dr. Richard O'Connor from Helena, Montana. I worked as a physician at St. Peter's Hospital for almost 30 years. I'm here with Joan Bird, who came along with me today to help out with this interview. If you want to introduce yourself, Joan, and just let people know you're there.

Dr. Joan Bird:

I'm the author of *Montana UFOs and Extraterrestrials*. I have a doctorate in zoology and a background in science. I have been a UFO researcher since 1999. I travel around the state giving talks about UFOs and continue to collect information. I always enjoy hanging out with people that are interested in this subject and that have good stories to tell.

Dr. Richard O'Connor:
Great, thanks. Keith, could you tell us what your history is as far as your work as a sheriff here in Montana?

Keith Wolverton:
I started in 1962 with what they call a sheriff's posse as a horseman. I pretty much grew up as a horseman and knew animals pretty well. I was just a special deputy then in 1962, and in 1964, I became employed by the Cascade County sheriff's office and I stayed there until the early 90s, I don't know exactly what year.

During the 70s, there was some strange things going on in Montana, strange things going on in Great Falls. I grew up in Great Falls. I was pretty interested in what was happening. I asked the sheriff, who was John Krsul at the time, [that] if he would give me about six weeks, I could probably solve this. But [that] was 40 years, six weeks ago, and I haven't solved anything yet.

During that period of time, people were seeing UFOs all over the place, including myself. I couldn't see anything as good as what I would like to have, nothing more than of a ball [of light] in the sky flying around. There was Bigfoot seen multiple times around this county, and cattle mutilations were going on, and that's what I really centered on, just trying to figure out who was killing the cattle, and I don't know the answer to it.

Dr. Richard O'Connor:

It's something we're all trying to figure out and hopefully, through this interview we'll get more information from you that will add to the data bank, [and] that people will become aware that the cattle mutilation phenomenon is still ongoing. It's real. It cannot be ascribed to natural predation as some groups have described.

Pete, can you tell us a little bit about your background with the sheriff's department in Teton County?

Pete Howard:

I was elected sheriff in 1974, November. I took office that same month and served until September of 1988, which at that time I had experienced heart surgery and opted to get out of the sheriff's office and went to the court system. I served 26 years as JP [justice of the peace]. So, I have 40 years of service with the county.

The first spring after I had been elected, as a matter of fact on Memorial Day of 1975, was the first reported cattle mutilation that we had had in our county. I think it was one of the very first ones in this whole geographic area.

I happened to be out of town at the time it happened. I talked to the undersheriff and the deputies, and they had the wisdom, at the instruction of the heifer owner, to bring in our local veterinarian to examine the heifer, which he did. He did a necropsy in the field. I don't know if any tissue or fluid tests were taken, I don't think they were. But his comments to the guys were, he had never seen anything like it in his life, meaning that after he opened the body cavity, the sexual organs had all been removed [and] part of the facial plate had been removed. I'm not sure about the nose or the lips at this time; it's been so many years ago.

But the entire situation was something that [the veterinarian] had never experienced before. And at that time, he was an experienced veterinarian, he was not right out of the vet school.

[The cattle mutilations] went on for another two and a half years in our county till about probably 1976, 1977, or something like that. At the same time, we started experiencing UFO sightings by people from various areas around our county.

In the meantime, I had made friends with Sheriff Krsul, who was Keith's sheriff at the time, and through that friendship, I was introduced to Keith and the other deputies down here. So, we had a team of people that we worked with during those years [with] good rapport. And like Keith says, unfortunately, 40 years later, here we are still wondering what had happened or what is happening.

But I'm a firm believer that it is something that is not attributable to human beings. I don't know who is responsible, but certainly it isn't something that a human being is capable of, I don't think.

I have had similar comments from different veterinarians. Probably over the time that we were doing this, we utilized at least five if not six or seven different veterinarians, and their opinions were pretty much the same, each time. They had never seen anything like it. They just hadn't.

The tests that we were able to run were very limited in scope, very amateurish, if you will, meaning basically Keith and I kind of did what we wanted to do. We did call the vets in, had them look and give us an opinion. The other thing that occurred, this started as I said on Memorial Day, by mid-summer that summer of 1975, it got very, very hot in July, August, September, so by the time some of these animals were discovered and reported to us, and when we got to them, the putrefaction of the bodies was so extreme that it was just really, really difficult to do any kind of an examination.

But historically, most of the [tissue] removal was the same. The face plate could be the right or left side of the face, the ears, the mouth, the lips, the nose, and the vaginal area, and it was predominantly performed on the female sex rather than the male sex of the cattle. We had one horse that was involved, and it was, I'm going to call it a mini horse, it was a pony as opposed to a full-grown horse. That one was a male, and we also had a mutilation reported on a Hereford bull. Otherwise, they're pretty much all younger cows, calf-bearing age and that kind of thing.

I didn't have in my county a Bigfoot sighting or report, all that happened down here with Keith in Cascade County. But we did simultaneously experience the UFO sightings and cattle mutilations, those kinds of things, and we worked together in trying to do what we could in those days. Keith was one of four deputies here in Cascade County that I cross-deputized. They were authorized to use deputy's arrest authority in my county if necessary, so for a continuing time, they were part of our group, if you will.

Dr. Richard O'Connor:

So, all of you cooperated in investigating these mutilations and you saw a number of these firsthand on the ground, I assume?

Keith Wolverton:
All of them on the ground. The horse that he's talking about was one of the most interesting ones we had ever done. I was there the day that we posted that animal out in the field and the veterinarian did it. And it had two holes in the jugular [vein]. We tried to figure out what would do that. We never came up with any answers but there was a lot of speculation that maybe, to keep the veins open, they would maybe put a saline solution in one [hole], pump [the blood] out the other, and the saline solution would keep the veins open. I think that was something the vet came up with. I certainly wouldn't have known that.

Dr. Richard O'Connor:
This has been a common description with a lot of these mutilations. These animals are found with their entire blood volume missing and no evidence of bleeding on the ground or even in snow, I've heard.

Keith Wolverton:
I found them in snow and I've never seen any blood.

Dr. Richard O'Connor:
Never saw any blood?

Keith Wolverton:
No. About that time, the one in the snow, we found the serrated cuts. That was the first time I had seen the serrated cuts, the first time I became aware of it, because it was so prominent. It may have been in other cattle too, but like Pete said, when you go out in July or August and look at the cow that has been laying there for two or three days, you don't really

want to spend a lot of time there. Things change, probably that serrated cut might change after a few days. We don't really know how many we had that had serrated cuts, but it was very prominent when we first noticed it.

Dr. Richard O'Connor:

In *Mystery Stalks the Prairie*, you show a detailed photograph of the serrated appearance of these hide incisions. You can see it has this very regular serrated appearance to the cut edge of the hide incision. Over here, Pete is holding a book written by Linda Moulton Howe called *An Alien Harvest.* Also, another excellent reference text for information about the cattle mutilation phenomenon. In that picture, I think you can also get a very good idea of how the serrations along the cut edge appear very regular, very unusual, and they appear to be cauterized as the cut was made.

One thing that I would like to point out is that this cut edge is not characteristic of any surgical instrument currently in use that I'm aware of in any operating room in the country. Basically, to make skin incisions, they use a Bard-Parker surgical steel blade, a Harmonic scalpel, or a Bovie electrocautery unit. Those three items are used to make virtually every single skin incision in any surgical procedure in this country.

I have personally witnessed probably 10,000 surgical incisions, and I've never seen an incision that looks like that [the serrated cuts]. So, this is being done with an instrument that is unknown to modern surgery. I think that's important to point out.

Pete, a few minutes ago you mentioned that you thought that these mutilation events could not be due to human activity. They're obviously being done by some intelligence that has a tremendous capability to subdue a huge, powerful animal. I've heard that this has happened with buffalo, elk, deer, pigs, goats, in various places around the world.

If we're talking about an intelligence that's responsible for this and it's not human, then this implies that our world is being affected, contacted in some way by some nonhuman intelligence. Do you agree with that?

Pete Howard:

I do, yeah. I guess, my own personal observation is just, these things are so neatly done, and you don't see it anywhere else. You being a medical doctor, if you say you haven't seen it, where does that take us? If you look at those, and I've had them in hand, we would excise around the wounds and recover that portion of the tissue or the hide, both Keith and I, and I don't know how many of those we looked at and examined, looked at them with just a small [magnifying] glass or a microscope. We're certainly not medical or scientific experts by any means, but it's just you don't see that kind of work anywhere else.

If you look at that closely, even in the picture, there are no hesitation marks as you would expect to see maybe if it were snip, snip, snip with a pair of pinking shears, something like that. I couldn't tell you how many days I spent in Great Falls looking for pinking shears of that size, style, and kind. You can't even cut a cow hide with a pair of pinking shears; it won't work, it just won't work. What those instruments were that were used, we don't have a clue, but it isn't something that we can say we can find another human being that has that ability. We don't have that ability, to my knowledge.

Dr. Richard O'Connor:

The other question it brings up is, how are these animals subdued? Are they anesthetized? And if they are anesthetized, then that implies the use of a drug. One thing that I think has slowed down our understanding of what's going on with this is the American Veterinary Medical Association's unwillingness to address this topic like a professional organization should.

One thing that should have been suggested long ago was to gain blood samples and tissue samples to check for the presence of any drugs that are commonly used, either in veterinary anesthesia or in modern medicine. I've looked for those studies and have not found any that were adequate, that really addressed how these animals are being subdued and subjected to these kinds of procedures. I think that's really an important question, and if the American Veterinary Medical Association was treating this subject with the seriousness that they should have been all along, than we would be much further down the line now in how we understand how this is being done and how these procedures are being carried out.

I would like to encourage veterinarians to go to the American Veterinary Medical Association and ask them to give up this ridiculous position that they have that's based on a study that was done by the FBI in 1979, that this is all due to animal predation. When both you Keith and you Pete and anybody that's looked at this, or maybe not had any personal experience but looked at it from reports of Linda Moulton Howe and others who have looked at this, there's no way that this is animal predation. It's absurd to suggest that.

I hope that the American Veterinary Medical Association, the Montana State Veterinary Medical Association, and other veterinary associations around our country will soon begin to address this like the professional organizations that they are, should.

Pete Howard:

Well, and in that same vein, this is cowboy country, where we live here in Montana. Of the animals that I viewed that were down, there was no sign of any struggle. There was never, ever any sign of someone on a horse, for instance, having roped the animal. They were just there. Just the carcass was there, no sign of struggle, no blood, on examination the body fluids are gone, the sexual parts and pieces are missing. It's unreal what was there, given what wasn't there. There was no sign of any other thing.

Keith mentioned he was born and raised with horses, so was I, I worked on a lot of ranches. If you're to go out here and put a rope on one of those cows, you're going to have some signs of struggle before that cow ever goes down, through whatever means. Whether you shoot them with a rifle or you put them down medically or whatever, there is going to be some signs of struggle. There was no such thing ever. There definitely was never ever, in any of the [mutilated] animals that I looked at, any sign of any kind of struggle. The carcass was just there, and the parts and pieces were missing.

Dr. Richard O'Connor:

I do have a couple of documents that I got off of the FBI website, it's vault.fbi.gov, regarding this conference that took place in Albuquerque. I think they had 13 mutilations on a reservation there in New Mexico. In this document it says, during this session of the conference, investigators from Arkansas pointed out that they have examined 28 cases of cattle mutilations, and it is their conclusion that all cases were the work of intentional mutilators and not of predators. That's on the FBI's website.

Then there was also, on that same website, a letter from Senator Floyd Haskell from the U.S. Senate. This was dated August of 1975 and was addressed to Theodore Roszak of the Denver office of the FBI. Senator Haskell wrote, the ranchers and rural residents of Colorado are concerned and frightened by these incidents. The bizarre mutilations are frightening in themselves. In virtually all the cases, the left ear, left eye, rectum, and sex organ of each animal has been cut away, and the blood drained from the carcass but with no traces of blood left on the ground and no footprints.

That's just an excerpt from that letter but that's certainly consistent with the description that you fellows have given us about what you encountered here in Montana. This was down in Colorado but essentially identical kinds of reports. These very stereotypical cuts along the face plate, the upper maxillary lip, the mandible, the ear missing, sometimes an eye missing, and then these sort of cookie-cutter cuts around the rectum and the vagina.

Keith Wolverton:

We took those cuts down to Colorado to have a pathologist look at them, and he didn't know what they were. He had no idea. He had never seen anything like it, so another dead end. All of the vets here looked at it, that we worked with, and we did have some really good veterinarians working with us. They would drop whatever they were doing, most of them, to just come out and meet us.

Pete Howard:
And the veterinaries that we utilized were large-animal vets, they weren't dog or cat vets. These guys made their living working with cattle and horses.

Dr. Richard O'Connor:
And they had no clue about what they were looking at?

Pete Howard:
No, they had never seen it.

Dr. Richard O'Connor:
Do you think that when they saw these things, they had the same feeling that you did that this could not have been done by humans, but they were just afraid to say it?

Keith Wolverton:
You see the on the front of this book here, there's a veterinarian standing right there with me. This is me and this Ken Anderson on the right. The veterinarian that was working with me the closest was there, and what I'm looking at is the fact that the lungs are displaced and moved away from the sidewalls of the steer. I can't remember if it's a steer or a cow. I think it was a cow.

There's no bruising, no hematoma, no nothing. So I asked the vet, why would this animal have the lungs tore away from its walls and not have some bruising? He says the only way that could happen, it got hit by a car, maybe, but that should cause bruising. He says, I suspect it's dropped. He says, that would be my theory.

Dr. Richard O'Connor:
I don't know if either one of you follow Linda Moulton Howe's website very closely, but recently she was reporting on these mutilations that happened in Kansas. She showed a photograph of a full-grown mutilated cow with its head stuffed down in a post hole. Now, if there are natural predators that are able to stuff a full-grown cow's head down into a post hole, I'll eat my hat.

I'm sure that both of you have spoken with Linda Howe and in my opinion, her website, earthfiles.com, is probably the best place to go for up-to-date information on the evolution of the cattle mutilation phenomenon and what's going on currently. I just want to take this opportunity to encourage everyone who sees this video to consider taking a look at Linda Moulton Howe's website and even subscribing to her website because that gives you access to many years of archive information. If you really want to understand this or learn more about it, that's a great place to go.

Pete Howard:
The different carcasses that we saw, when I would leave the ranch property, I would always tell the animal owner, watch the animal if you can and let me know if you see anything come around it. Well, in our area we have, first of all, grizzly bears. We have lots of coyotes, we have hundreds of magpies, crows, that kind of thing. These [mutilated] animals were not subject to predation; they lay there and literally rotted away. Nothing ever ate them; nothing ever latched onto them and drug them, such as a grizzly bear. The opportunity for predation [in this area] was extreme, [but] I never, ever saw it.

Keith took a lot of heat from the fellow that was the head of the Montana Stock Growers Association about that very thing, that everything that happened was all due to predators. That's absolutely not the way it was. Whether he ever went to one of these sites or not and looked at an animal, I don't have a clue. I would like to think maybe he did not, because he certainly was uninformed as far as I'm concerned. But that was his comment around the state. He made a lot of noise without ever having much knowledge. [He] never offered to come up and visit with Keith and I; [he] didn't say, well, next time you have a report, call me, we will try and get there. He just had an opinion and an attitude, that was it.

Keith Wolverton:
Those two calves we had up there that night, one in the water and something drug it out of the water. No tracks, and had a little incision on it, and all of the innards were sitting up on top of the calf. How did they do that?

Pete Howard:
It had walked from grassland down to a lake. This is, what am I trying to say, not a reservoir, just a pothole. It had just rained and that's what made it. But it was really muddy, so the cattle all used the same path to get down to the water. These two heifers were together, and they got down to the water, and you could see that, and then they were laid over. It was like you reached out with a big hook and just literally slid them back, and no tracks of any kind, and they were back from the water probably 20 or 30 yards, something like that.

Dr. Richard O'Connor:
So a long way and no tracks?

Pete Howard:
There wasn't even a bird track around, much less a human or a vehicle or anything like that. Absolutely nothing.

Keith Wolverton:
And we never saw any more like that.

Dr. Richard O'Connor:
Was there a skid?

Pete Howard:
Skid marks, yeah.

Keith Wolverton:
Yeah, you could see the [skid] marks.

Pete Howard:
You could see skid marks in the mud until it hit kind of dry ground. It wasn't dry but it was drier than where it had left the track. It was just really weird.

We did look at a couple of natural deaths. This summer, we've had a lot of lightning, we've had cattle killed and horses killed from lightning strikes. It happens every year. Those kinds of things go on from year to year, but for the most part, the ones that we're calling mutilations, that's where something very, very unusual caused the death of those calves and that horse that we saw.

Keith Wolverton:
I think probably the last one that I looked at, not too long before I retired so that would have put it in the 80s. Square Butte out here, there was a rancher there and he called me out

to look at this cow. He says, I've got a cow out here, it's kind of laying in a funny position, and it's dead. I knew this guy and I went out there. This cow was laying on its back, all four legs straight up in the air, and the bag [udder] is cut out in a perfect circle, gone.

So I called a vet who lives out there. No, he did, the rancher called a vet, one that I've never used. I called the vet and asked him, when he goes out there, if he would call me and let me know. Yeah, he said. Several days go by and I never hear from him, so I call him up and I say, did you have a look at that cow? He said, yeah. Did you find anything unusual? He says no. Well, he says, there was one thing kind of unusual. I say, what's that? He says, well, she was pregnant, [and] the calf was gone. I say, you didn't find that unusual? There you go. There's a difference between some veterinarians and other veterinarians. He didn't want to believe it.

Dr. Richard O'Connor:
Keith, do you have a particular recollection about an interesting case that you would like to tell us about?

Keith Wolverton:
It's not a case, it just was a happening. I was returning probably 11:30 at night from Missoula and I was in the area of Simms. To my left, there's a cliff which drops down into Sun River. This orange ball came flying off that cliff, went right in front of our car, and gone. I would say that this thing traveled a period of maybe eight miles, 10 miles, in like four seconds. I couldn't draw a line across the window as quick as that thing was going.

I had Kenny Anderson with me, he was our photographer. We both saw it. But that very same day, this gentleman [*in-*

dicating Howard] had a guy up on Freezeout Lake see a UFO kind of attach itself to a bomb run. What kind of planes were those?

Pete Howard:
B-1s, B-52s.

Keith Wolverton:
This guy took his rifle and his scope and put it right up there on top [of his truck] so he can get a good look at this craft, and I think the rest of the story is yours, you made some phone calls.

Pete Howard:
It's a long story. I'll do it. Do you want to do that now or do you want to get an overview?

Dr. Richard O'Connor:
Sure. Go ahead.

Pete Howard:
A detachment from Louisiana was assigned to Montana to set up a portable electronic bombing range. This is the Air Force. I don't remember the exact year, I'm going to say 1976, 1978, in there somewhere. The little town that it was near [probably Pendroy], it was north of where I live, it's near the north boundary of Teton County. So they set the unit up and I guess they were 20, 25, maybe 30 Air Force personnel assigned to it. The bombers would come to the area from out of state, North Dakota or wherever. Predominantly, they were B-52s and B-1s. They would contact the station and get whatever information they shared with them.

They would make the bombing run west toward the [Rocky Mountain Front], and then their exit was to make a turn right on the mountain front, and come east again. Usually, the outbound track would take them over a place that we call locally Freezeout Lake, a fish and game corner there. *(Editor's note: Freezeout Lake is a state wildlife management area.)*

So this gentleman Keith was referring to was a Fish, Wildlife & Parks' employee. He was going home for the evening, it was about 5 o'clock, so he left the parking lot from Fish, Wildlife & Parks property, stopped for traffic coming on the highway, and while he was stopped, something caught his attention in the peripheral vision on his left-hand side.

He looked up and here is the bomber, B-1, B-52 or whatever, flying, and usually, they would be outbound at around 500 or 600 foot [altitude]. This was a low-level run. Right above it at the tail and slightly behind it was a saucer-style UFO, and it followed that aircraft until it was out of sight from the fellow that was observing all this.

So he came to town, drove up in front of the sheriff's office, and it was 5 o'clock, a little after, and by then I'm ready to go home, too. He just sat in his pickup for a few minutes and collected himself, and pretty quick here he came in. He was just almost white, couldn't talk, he just was out of himself. We sat him down, got him a cup of coffee, got him going, and he related the story of what he had just seen. It just scared the pants off him.

That was the one and only occasion that we had with those bombers that were flying in and out, but it was pretty a significant situation to this fellow that viewed that. Keith, didn't you pull that off the Freedom of Information Act later, some of the particulars on that?

Keith Wolverton:

I think I didn't, but somebody did that I worked with from back East, I can't remember his name. Greenwood maybe. He had sent me some stuff on that, and all the radar went out. I think it was—

Pete Howard:

The radar equipment on the aircraft going outbound was disabled during the time. Of course, we made a record of date, time, location, and all that, and from that, I guess, that matched up with the time that was recorded by the aircraft of what had happened to them. It apparently disabled most of the electronics on that aircraft for a period of whatever time, I don't know. That's pretty unique.

[The witness] called it a UFO; he said a flying saucer. When he described it, he gave the physical description of the saucer that we all know from the media, that kind of thing. That's what he was referring to as the saucer style as opposed to the mothership or the cigar-shape thing.

Dr. Richard O'Connor:

That event—

Pete Howard:

Before all this other stuff had happened, I had met the [Air Force] officer in charge. I want to say he was a colonel; it doesn't make any difference. They used to host quarterly meetings for the sheriffs in Great Falls at Malmstrom Air Force Base, and I always tried to come down and have lunch, meet the guys, and talk to them as most of the other sheriffs in the area did.

I met this [officer] when we visited and he said, well, we

understand you guys are trying to find these UFOs and track them and do all these things in the evening hours. He said, if it happens again, why don't you give us a call and if we're not doing something else and our equipment's available, we'll try and zero in and see if we can find these on our equipment.

So the evening that this incident happened, a friend of mine, a retired schoolteacher, drove into my office about 9 o'clock at night, and it was in the fall of the year sometime. It was dark by then. He walked in and he said, have you looked outside your window? I said no, so I looked off to the south and west. There's this bright light up in the sky and he said, that's too big for a star and it's too close and whatever. I said, well, why don't you get in my car and make sure you have your seat belt on because we're going to go do a visit.

We beat feet at 100 miles an hour plus down the highway. We're going probably 12, 15 miles as the crow flied to the approximate location where this bright light was. On my way out the door, I asked the dispatcher to call the Pendroy [Air Force] tracking station and tell the officer in charge there that we were onto something and could he see if he can track it.

So down the road we go, and we turn off the highway and we're flying down a graveled road.... So this light, for the two of us in the car, it stayed about the same intensity and size, then all of a sudden looked like, well, it's moving away from us.

At about that time, we get a phone call from the office and they said, the colonel or whatever called and said they have locked onto an object. They don't know what it is, but it is in the area you're talking about. [My friend] says, oh, we can still see the light, and we think we're maybe five miles from it, something like that. So we drove. All of a sudden, the light goes out. I called the office and I said, well, we no longer have a light.

They said, well, the tracking station said they can still see it and it's moving in a northeast direction and not at high speed. And they gave me the speed and I don't remember what it was, like 15, 20, 30 miles an hour or something like that. It went on for a few minutes. Then, on the law enforcement radio—[*turning to Wolverton*] I forget whether all four of you guys were in the same car too.

Keith Wolverton:
Glenn Osborne and I were in the car. We should've been right under it.

Pete Howard:
We all have the same radio system. Keith and his sheriff at the time and Kenny and Arnie?

Keith Wolverton:
I don't know if they were out or not, I can't remember.

Pete Howard:
I can't remember either. They get on the radio and they said, Howard, where are you at, we're getting in on this. So I told them. As it turned out, we met on the highway, and the colonel had called and he said, you need to come up here. He said, I got something on the scope, and you need to see it. If you can, come on up. I called these guys and told them, and we went to Pendroy. We went in this trailer, and normally the equipment in there would be staffed by one person. Well, the colonel was so excited about what he had seen, he had two sets of eyes on every machine. He had called out extra people to visualize what they're watching.

There's a scroll similar to a polygraph, and that scroll was telling them the distance from the radar site to where it was over the ground. It told them the altitude above the ground. It told them the speed, what else, I can't I remember if anything else. But [the colonel] said, here's the unique part of it.

We're looking at the scroll and [the object] is coming across at a fairly steady [altitude], just a little bit of a waiver in it, and then all of a sudden [*Howard quickly lifts his hand and makes a whistling sound*], it goes straight up, instantaneous stop, and then it starts floating again. I said, my goodness, what do you suppose that is? The colonel looked me right in the eye and he says, You know, we do not have a clue. We don't have anything that can fly like that. It gained 6,000 or 8,000 or 10,000 feet of altitude just almost instantaneously, stopped, and then started just drifting again.

Dr. Richard O'Connor:
Wow.

Pete Howard:
Pretty unique. And then, it wasn't long after that and here come a couple of cars of security guys. They came in and ushered us out, took the scroll with them, and that was the end of playtime.

Keith Wolverton:
As I recall, they said that they would have somebody from the Pentagon call you or something, the next day.

Pete Howard:
Yeah. The next day I sit there, and I waited, waited, and waited, no call. I thought, well, no sense getting in a hurry, this is the government we're dealing with.

Dr. Joan Bird:
What did the guys look like that came in? Were they wearing uniforms?

Pete Howard:
Well, yes, but it wasn't an Air Force uniform, it was like black coveralls, I must say. They had a uniform of their own. There was three or four of them, and they had long metal tubes and they rolled the scrolls up into the tubes, and they went out the door. They came in their car with blackened windows and down the road they went. It was pretty unique.

And then the next day, I finally called the base commander in Great Falls and I said, we were going to get a phone call, and nobody's called. Well, we're just doing a little debriefing amongst ourselves, but somebody will be calling you. Okay, so I sat there again that day, did other things waiting for the phone call. The short story is, I never did get a debriefing call from anybody.

Dr. Richard O'Connor:
Keith, I'm on page 55 of *Mystery Stalks the Prairie*, you wrote that deputy Arnie Sands interviewed a sergeant who was stationed at an ICBM missile site near Vaughn, Montana, and was told by that sergeant that a UFO hovered over the controlled airspace of that nuclear missile site, taking the form of a large and a very brilliant light through which he could not determine a shape, and was also not accompanied by the sound of a helicopter.

That report is consistent with, and you may be familiar with Captain Robert Salas, who has also told us about incidents where UFOs have hovered over nuclear missile sites and actually turned off our nuclear missiles on numerous occasions, apparently. This April of 2016, Mr. Robert Hastings, a UFO researcher, produced a documentary film called *UFOs and Nukes: The Secret Link Revealed*, in which he interviews, I think, four or five different previous United States Air Force officers who were also stationed at various nuclear missile installations and who have also testified that they were present when these UFO events occurred, and our nuclear missiles were rendered inoperable, basically.

Keith Wolverton:

It was in '67 that Robert Salas was involved and that's what he talks about. I got involved in one in '76. In the Lewistown area, a giant craft hovered right over the top of the missile silo, the headquarters—what do they call it—the large control facilities. Everybody was down deep [in the underground silo] except the guys up on [the surface] watching guard. This craft came down and they notified everybody down below what was going on. They all went upstairs and looked at this craft. It was right there.

They notified Malmstrom; Malmstrom called the Air National Guard [in Great Falls]; and two jets were sent down there immediately. This was October, November. As [the jets] approached that missile site, the craft just went straight up in the air and jets went through it. [*Wolverton uses his hands to show the UFO rising straight up and the jets flying below it.*] The jets just came back around and apparently didn't see anything. After they had [gone] back, the craft came down on top of the missile silo. This was kept kind of secret.

One of the officers—I shouldn't say he was an officer, he would not identify himself, but he was on the site that night—came into my office and he wanted to talk to me. He wouldn't divulge his name or his rank, he just said, I want you to know I was there, and it happened. I say, what happened? He described everything I just told you to me in detail. Apparently, there's some numbers on the computer that controls where these missiles are going to go, and all those numbers were changed.

Dr. Richard O'Connor:
Wow.

Keith Wolverton:
I thought that was interesting. I would like to have known what they were changed to, but I never did find out or what they were to begin with.

Dr. Joan Bird:
I haven't heard that one before. That's very interesting.

Keith Wolverton:
It's pretty classified, I would say. If there is a number to go to a certain spot, and they were all changed, what does it mean?

Dr. Joan Bird:
Yes, I'd like to know what they changed them to.

Keith Wolverton:
And then when it left, they reset everything. But it really happened, and it was huge. It covered the whole launch control facility, lights, just lit up.

The period of time that we were working on this, I got very involved with Malmstrom Air Force Base and I found them to be more than helpful. They supplied me with night vision goggles, they would answer any questions we had for them.

One night we had a flap going on with sightings going on all over, and they even had one of our deputies go out to, I guess it was their radar unit, and watch what was going on. So they invited us out to see that. People might think that the military might know what's going on, but if they do, as my friend told me, [they are] much higher than he is, and he was the commander of the space out here. So, he doesn't know.

Dr. Richard O'Connor:
Well, that's good to know that it's not everybody in the military that's been responsible for covering this up. But I think, from what I've learned about it, I've come to the conclusion that there's definitely been some subset of the "government" that has been involved in trying to dissuade people from looking at this. At least, that's my conclusion.

Keith Wolverton:
For the reason of Malmstrom being in Great Falls, I just want people to know they were cooperative.

Dr. Richard O'Connor:
Good to know.

Keith Wolverton:
I don't know about the rest of the military. I'm sure there are some cover-ups that they don't want us to know about. But there's been a lot of books written about military people seeing a lot of strange craft, and they all come in different sizes and shapes, like I was talking about before.

The most interesting one that I can think of that was fairly recent, say, within the last 10 years, a rancher who lives straight south of here. His wife gets off work at midnight, and she picked up her mother, and [they] drove to the ranch.

As they're driving out to the Eden country—there's a big turn in the road and it's a right hand turn down a gravel road and another right hand turn into their ranch—something came down on top of her car, hovered right above it, and she's driving, probably 55 to 70 miles an hour, she wasn't sure. The sides of the road were lit up and the grass was moving.

She made that first right-hand turn, and the craft went right with her, it never varied one bit, it stayed right on top of her and made the same right-hand turn. The next right-hand turn she made into the ranch, it made a left-hand turn. And this lasted for several miles.

Dr. Richard O'Connor:
Wow.

Keith Wolverton:
She didn't hear any sound, any whirring sound—she thought it was a helicopter because what else could it be? But this ranch has had a history of other strange things going on. We talked about the cow with the head in a post hole, this guy had a steer, and its horn was stuck so far in the ground, the deputy who went out and looked at it had to have help to pull it out.

Dr. Richard O'Connor:
It's hard to imagine how that would happen unless the animal had been dropped from a height.

Keith Wolverton:
Exactly. That's the only thing we could think of. Same way

with the cow with the head in the post hole, how do you get that jammed in there. You can't take a steer and jam his head and put the horns in the hole, it just doesn't work that way. So I'm sure it was dropped. The more I think about it over the years, I'm sure most of these cattle were dropped. However, sometimes you find them under a tree. How do they get there? This one with the serrated cut was covered almost [by a tree], and there was snow on the trees which didn't fall off, and so there was pretty good protection underneath that tree, from being dropped. So, I don't think it was dropped, that one. I think something else happened to it.

Pete Howard:

I got a call early one—was it the same day or the next day—it doesn't make any difference, I guess. A family had been in Great Fall shopping: man, wife, and two or three kids. They got home, it was dark, and there was a cigar ship, I'm going to call it a mothership, if you will, stationed over the driveway into their home. The house was located probably a quarter a mile off the secondary highway. So, they stopped short of going even onto their own driveway.

And then finally, they went on to the house, got out. The ship simply moved to the west a little bit and gave them some space. They got out of the car and went in the house. The gentleman had a pair of binoculars. I don't remember if they purchased them that day or they were laying there immediately accessible. He looked at it for a while out the window, he, his wife, and the kids did. Finally, he said, well, I'm going to go out and see if I can get close to it to get a good look at it.

He left the kitchen area, went outside, and as he tried to get closer to it, it started moving, and it would just simply evade, if you will. It backed up enough, not high speed, about the same speed as he was walking. So he finally just made up your mind, I'm just going to keep at it and see if I can wear it out and get to it.

If you go south from his house, it's about a quarter a mile to the highway and from the highway south to the Sun River is a distance of maybe a half a mile, and then [the terrain] drops down into the river bottom. He followed that ship that distance.

In the meantime, there was a colony, if you will, I don't remember how many in number, three or four or five maybe more, of smaller disc-size ships that were coming and going out of the underneath of this mothership or this cigar-shaped thing. It finally got over the river valley and just simply disappeared over the edge of the hill and that was the last he saw of it. But both he, his wife, and the kids, all had a really good look at it. It's pretty interesting talking to them. I think Arnie did a polygraph on that one even.

Keith Wolverton:
I don't remember. I just remember you and I talking to him and he just was very honest.

Pete Howard:
I guess that's the other thing maybe that's important for this tape. The people that we've talked to, that I talked to, whether it's mutilation, UFOs or whatever, they're just good common people. They're not kooks, they didn't make outlandish statements, they weren't looking for any press, never any mention of money for the stories, any of that kind of thing. Just, hey, this is what I saw, will you come and listen and let me tell you about it. They're just good, solid, sound people.

I probably didn't know the difference but I'm going to say I didn't listen to any kooks, if there are any out there. I talked to a lot of people over the years, both with the UFOs and the mutilations, and they're just good solid people.

Dr. Richard O'Connor:
That's important to point out.

Pete Howard:
Yeah. They're not people looking for notoriety or anything like that.

Dr. Richard O'Connor:
You often hear people say, well, the only people that see those things are kooky people and I don't think that's true at all.

Pete Howard:
In those days, we didn't have cell phones and all that kind of thing, so for the most part, during the daylight hours, some people are packing cameras but a lot of other times at different hours of the day, there were no cameras. So you have so much more media, if you will, available today than we had back then. So a lot of things they were telling us, they didn't have any way of substantiating them through pictures because a lot of it was nighttime occurrences.

The other one, and this is real classic, this is my favorite of all of them I did. We got a report about 6:30, 7 o'clock in the evening and it's a fall night, I do remember that. About a 60 mile-an-hour wind, and dirty, dusty, cold. One of our county commissioners was out east to Dutton, so he gets over there—and the county commissioners had their own little radio system that was connected to the road department system. We couldn't talk directly to them. I could talk to them through my office, but I couldn't talk car to car.

So the commissioner gets to Dutton and he has a sighting, and he's pretty excited. He tells them what he sees, and I go out and get in the car and I head out for Dutton. This is a distance of 20, 25 miles, something like that. When I get over there, he said, it left, it's just gone. He said, I'm on my way home. He gets home and I thought, well, I'll go out and visit with him to see what he did see.

So I get to the house and he and his wife are there, nobody else, and the kitchen table is just covered with paperwork, and she's just frantic. She's going through looking at things and the commissioner is standing there, and he's kind of laughing and giggling. I said, well, what's so funny here? What did you see? Did you tell your wife? Well, yeah, he said. She's looking to see if my life insurance policies cover me being taken by a UFO. And that's what she was doing.

Dr. Richard O'Connor:
She was serious?

Pete Howard:
She was serious. She was looking through his insurance policy. Anyhow, the sighting he saw, he called it a disc. It was probably like a minute; he didn't have it in view that long. It was later, I think, that same night when my old buddy, [sheriff] John Krsul called and told me that he just rented a helicopter. He was going to run it down with a helicopter or know the reason why. Well, luckily, it was blowing so hard the private helicopter services wouldn't fly.

Dr. Richard O'Connor:
That's probably a good day.

Pete Howard:
And the last one, south of Chouteau about two miles, three miles, something like that, there's twin buttes, Priest Butte and Rattlesnake Butte. A family lived in their home between the buttes and this lady gets up in the morning, makes coffee. She's standing in the kitchen, looking out the window over the sink toward Rattlesnake Butte, which is the one farthest west and it's a distance of a half a mile, maybe a little bit more. It's daylight but just breaking day. Well, here's the mothership, just hovering, if you will, in a little natural depression up on the side hill, and saucer-type ships are flying in and around and over the top and going around the hill and back again, going in and out of the belly of the mothership.

Then she wakes up her husband and he gets up, and they watch this together for half an hour. Finally, in their visitation between themselves, they decided to call me, but she said, are you busy, can you come out? She didn't say what she was looking for or looking at, and I wasn't bright enough to ask her. I just said, yeah, I'll be right there. So I got dressed and went out.

Unfortunately, I drove right by where this had been, it turns out. It left before I got there but I didn't know where it was going and what I might've been looking for or looking at. But the two of them, they gave a pretty explicit description of what they saw. They called it a cigar-shaped mothership because of the entry and exits of the little guys in the bottom of it. She said, it went out of sight by going west around the hill, and then because of the hill it was gone.

Dr. Richard O'Connor:
Was she fairly close to it?

Pete Howard:
Half a mile or about that distance from her house.

Dr. Richard O'Connor:
Pretty close.

Pete Howard:
Every time I go down that road, I think of it and I look at the hill, and I go, boy, I wish you'd come back. That'd be quite a view.

Dr. Joan Bird:
And that was the Pearson case?

Pete Howard:
Yes. That one, they never had a reoccurrence. Farm people, just good, solid people, and the first thing in the morning, that's what you woke up to.

Dr. Richard O'Connor:
A lot of people when they look at stuff, especially on the internet, they're very suspicious about whether what they're hearing is the truth. It's something that's becoming more and more difficult. I've noticed myself. It's becoming more and more difficult, when we look at stuff on the internet, to know if we are listening to the truth. Having listened to the two of you present this material, I have no doubt that you're telling us, in a very truthful way, about these experiences that you had. I'm assuming that that's a fact. Correct?

Pete Howard:
Yeah.

Keith Wolverton:
Yeah, I certainly don't think anybody ever lied to me about it.

Pete Howard:
I never felt that anybody was setting me up. I do pretty good interviews. I think I have the ability to pull that out of somebody if they're not being truthful. I never, ever felt that way about the people I talked to, they were just good people.

Dr. Richard O'Connor:
One other question just to alleviate any skeptics' minds, I called the two of you and asked you to participate in this and you just readily agreed to do so. You have no financial incentive for doing this; you have no other reason to do this other than you both have had some unique experiences in your careers as sheriffs getting calls, fielding calls, that most of 99.9% of us wouldn't get.

I just want to make it clear that nobody is being paid for this, nobody is going to realize any financial gain from participating in this interview. We're just doing this so that people can know about some of these experiences and understand that there are events going on in the sky and events going on on the ground and have been going on for decades now, and people need to be aware of it. They need to pay attention to it. Because I think that, as more and more people begin to incorporate this into their worldview, we'll begin making faster progress towards figuring all this out and eventually leading to some better understanding of what all this is that's happening and why it's happening.

Keith Wolverton:
If we were talking about people perpetrating a hoax, I just don't believe it happened. I think everything that I saw and talked to was something. But it brings me to mind, one night, Sheriff Osborne and myself received a call that there was something going on out towards Simms and we should be out there. There was a lady out there who was babysitting and there was something hovering over her house. Glenn and I got there pretty fast. I think we both probably got out of bed. I did this many, many times, get out of bed, get dressed, and go.

When I got out there, I found, I think it was three children and the babysitter hiding in a huge rock fireplace and genuinely afraid, scared. They watched this craft. This is a hotel size. This is huge. They had given me a size. I don't recall right now what it was, but it could have been 300 feet long. It was tremendously big. It had a row of windows across the top and a row of windows across the bottom, and it just floated. It went over the house and then floated right along the ground. She said it went over and up that road that goes through a big ranch out there. It used to be, Newman?

Pete Howard:
Hamilton.

Keith Wolverton:
Hamilton Ranch. Glenn and I left them, and we waited until, I think, the parents came home and sat with them. Then we took a drive up that road and we spent a lot of time just listening and looking, and probably traveled maybe 20 miles around. We never saw anything. However, Glenn seemed to

think something happened that night. I said, what? Well, he says, something was wrong.

I say, well, in what way? He says, I don't know. He says, timewise, things didn't add up for me. I didn't know what that meant to him. Usually, when I left somewhere, I would keep track of my time so I didn't lose any time because a lot of people [in reported UFO incidents] lose time, apparently. My car never ever quit running, which seems to be a story that people [in UFO incidents] will tell you, my car just quit.

Dr. Richard O'Connor:
I heard that before.

Keith Wolverton:
I never had that problem. I thought that story was interesting to know why anybody would perpetrate a hoax like that and then you get out there and find them hiding in a—

Dr. Richard O'Connor:
In a fireplace.

Keith Wolverton:
In a fireplace. And very sincere, the kids were all scared. Of course [the babysitter] was scared, which made the kids scared. But that was not too long after Pete's story about a pony, and it's not very far away....

Pete Howard:
I guess the important thing for me in relating what I have told you, for people to know and understand, that I myself saw one instance, and that was the bright light that we chased that they did catch with the radar thing. Whatever it was, I don't know, we never saw a shape, just the light. When the

light went out, that was it. All of the other incidents are the things that other people experienced and told me. Like I said, I have just a lot of faith in their integrity, their veracity, no reason to believe that they were lying to me, none at all.

As far as your comment on, are we being paid? No, certainly. My idea of the whole thing is just that when Keith and I were working, that's why we took pictures, that's why we wrote reports, it's for posterity. It's, hey, you make a record of what you do, you are public servants, first of all.

We're individuals too, and we are now for sure, but you record these things and as far as I'm concerned, everything that I left behind in my office is public record. I did it on county time, I was paid for it with county money, anybody that wants to see that, if the sheriff will allow them, can go and see it, it's not anything at all that's secure or has some kind of security attachment to it.

Dr. Richard O'Connor:
Would some of those things be photographs that you took of some of the cattle mutilations?

Pete Howard:
Yes, there's photographs and reports, different notes, different letters. Different people would write a little letter and send it in so I may have to call. Instead of calling me or seeing me on the road and talking to me, they'd send me a letter and say, hey, did you know? And then I contact them and go that route. But there's just different things that we collected and put into preservation, if you will.

Dr. Richard O'Connor:
Right. Good.

End of interview